DISCOVERING DRAMA

Theory and Practice for the Primary School

Paula Murphy and Margaret O'Keeffe

GILL & MACMILLAN

Gill & Macmillan
Hume Avenue
Park West
Dublin 12
with associated companies throughout the world
www.gillmacmillan.ie

ISBN–13: 978 0 7171 3934 7
ISBN–10: 0 7171 3934 4

Index compiled by Cover to Cover
Print origination in Ireland by Carrigboy Typesetting Services, Co. Cork

*The paper used in this book is made from the wood pulp of managed forests.
For every tree felled, at least one is planted, thereby renewing natural resources.*

A catalogue record is available for this book from the British Library.

DISCOVERING DRAMA

TO JARI, DAISY AND
THE O'KEEFFE FAMILY

TO GERRY, OLIVIA
AND THE MURPHY FAMILY

CONTENTS

ACKNOWLEDGMENTS

We would like to thank the following people for their support throughout the development and writing of this book: ADEI (Association of Drama in Education in Ireland), Jim Coleman, Aine Cregan, Hazel Dunphy, Michael Finnernan, Colm Hefferon, Mary Howard, Celia Keenan, Margaret Leahy, Mark Morgan, Paul Murphy, John McArdle, Teresa O Doherty, Peter O'Driscoll, Michael O Maolcatha, Team Educational Theatre Company and Dennis Twoomey.

We would like to acknowledge the funding received from Mary Immaculate College and St Patrick's College, Drumcondra.

We would also like to express our sincere thanks to the principals, staff and pupils of the following schools: St Brigid's G.N.S, Killester, Dublin; St Bridgit's N.S, Singland, Limerick; Mary Mother of Hope N.S, Clonee, County Meath; Scoil Mologa, Harolds Cross, Dublin and Scoil Naomh Eoin, Lispole, County Kerry, Tarrane National School Kilkelly, Co. Mayo.

Finally, we would like to dedicate this book to our families and friends for their support and encouragement throughout this process.

INTRODUCTION

> **YOLLAND:** . . .*The day I arrived in Ballybeg . . . the moment you brought me in here, I had a curious sensation . . . It was a momentary sense of discovery; no – not quite a sense of discovery . . . a sense of recognition, of confirmation of something I half knew instinctively; as if I had stepped . . .*
>
> **OWEN:** *Back into ancient time?*
>
> **YOLLAND:** *No, no. It wasn't an awareness of direction being changed but of experience being of a totally different order.*
>
> Extract from *Translations* by Brian Friel, Act 2

Ireland boasts a long and varied tradition of theatrical endeavour, which arguably includes some of the world's finest playwrights, actors and dramatists. Throughout its colourful history, it has represented the variety of ways in which theatre can powerfully engage its audience, and indeed influence the society within which it operates. It has been a medium for entertainment, for representation, for literary endeavour and for political change. Whether one reflects on the melodrama of Boucicault, the innovations of the early Abbey Theatre, the literary genius of playwrights such as J.M. Synge, Seán O'Casey, Samuel Beckett, Brian Friel and Tom Murphy, or the ongoing theatrical and literary experimentation of the current Irish theatre scene – the desire to engage and challenge audiences on an intellectual, emotional and artistic level has been a passionate commitment for all.

Despite this rich tradition, it has taken some time for the relevance and potentially profound impact of drama in our educational system to be formally recognised. During the last thirty years particularly, many innovative teachers, drama facilitators and theatre-in-education practitioners have supported, modelled and challenged drama practice in Irish schools. Indeed it is their commitment, vision and success that have finally led to the formal introduction of drama to the newly-revised curriculum, and to the writing of this book. As teachers, the introduction of drama to the curriculum presents us with a profound opportunity and indeed a profound challenge. It presents us with the opportunity to enhance and invigorate our approach to teaching and to the arts, and with the challenge of re-imagining what we teach and how we teach it. This book seeks to support teachers, student teachers, and all those involved in the teaching of drama, with comprehensive, practical and theoretical guidance in the area of process drama, which is the basis of the new drama curriculum.

What Is Process Drama?

While we aim in this book to represent the wide range of theatre-related experience available to the child – from the spontaneous play of the young infant to the more formal experience of attending or performing in a theatre production – our emphasis is on a particular approach to the teaching of drama known as process drama. The title which is given to this well-established practice in both teaching and theatre circles may take different forms which one will recognise from other literature on the subject, namely drama-in-education, educational drama, participatory theatre and learning through theatre. In any case, what is central to process drama is a recognition of the social, artistic and educational qualities of theatre, alongside a desire to experiment with its traditional form, so that these qualities can be explored, experienced and manipulated by young people in an active and imaginative way.

While process drama has its roots in theatre form, it is essentially improvisational in nature. This means that children do not follow a predetermined script, even though many of the elements of theatre are employed during the experience. As in theatre, they explore a fictional situation which has some thematic relevance to their lives. They employ a range of theatre conventions and elements to explore this fiction, and they manipulate time during the exploration rather than follow a linear plot. However, the fundamental distinction between a process drama and the performance of a traditional play, is that the fiction in a process drama is just a shell, or a stimulus for exploration. Rather than being determined in advance, it is developed by the children themselves during the process. It is motivated not by the need to create an interesting story for its own sake, but to explore more meaningfully a particular facet of human experience.

The traditional notion of audience is also redefined in process drama in that there are no separate spectators to the activity. Instead children become an active and responsible 'audience' to their own work. The teacher does not act as a director in the traditional sense, but employs the principles of the dramatist to facilitate the process from the inside. While she initiates and supports the drama in a variety of ways, her overall aim is to balance the need for play, improvisation and spontaneity, on the one hand with the need for dramatic structure and thematic focus on the other.

▶ *Process Drama: Philosophical Perspectives*

In order to understand the principles highlighted above more fully, it is helpful to consider how process drama relates both to theatre and to education and how it emerged from innovations in both fields. Because it is beyond the scope of this introduction to trace the entire story of the development of process drama, the basis for its philosophical development will be given precedence over historical detail.

Let us first begin by reflecting on a child's experience of a visit to the theatre. There is much to attract the teacher to organising such an event for children. A theatre performance is based fundamentally on the notion of story. It presents a person or group of people in a particular context, who we gradually get to know through a series of episodes. It usually focuses on a particular theme or question related to real life, and it is presented in a form which is not only artistically and visually engaging, but conducive to creating empathy. As such, the experience of watching a play would seem to embody very powerfully many of the most fundamental principles of effective teaching, and have much to offer developments in educational practice. It is our belief that all children should attend a variety of theatre performances in their primary school years. However, while acknowledging this, practitioners from both fields have also argued strongly for a much more active role for the participant in the theatre encounter, and indeed for an overall re-evaluation of the form within which it can take place.

▶ *An Educational Perspective*

In educational circles it might be argued that the experience of being an audience member, while very engaging and challenging for the child, does not go far enough in terms of his active participation in the event. Their concerns might include questions such as the following. *Why is the child watching instead of doing? Or, What influence does he have over the content or direction of this piece?* Such critical reflection represents a passionate commitment to a teaching approach which relies fundamentally on the active participation of the child, and has its roots in constructivist and progressive educational philosophies. Within this perspective, which is influenced by leading theorists such as Dewey, Vygotsky, Bruner and Freire, the child is viewed as an active meaning maker, rather than a vessel to be filled with decontextualised facts and pieces of information. He creates his own meanings through his ongoing interaction with other people and with his environment, and learns best through problem-solving approaches, which simultaneously stimulate his intellectual, emotional and physical capabilities. Paulo Freire represents the urgency which is felt in a variety of educational contexts with regard to the above principles, when he argues that,

> *Liberation is praxis . . . Those truly committed to the cause of liberation can accept neither the mechanistic concept of consciousness as an empty vessel to be filled, nor the use of banking methods of domination (propaganda, slogans-deposits) in the name of liberation.*
>
> (Freire, 1970, p. 60)

▶ *A Theatre Perspective*

Critical questions with regard to the traditional *form* of a theatrical encounter have also emerged within the theatre itself, particularly during the 60s and 70s. Directors and practitioners such as Bertolt Brecht and Augusto Boal, in their recognition of the inherent political and pedagogical power of theatre, were also concerned about its potential to manipulate and control audiences. This was due to its unparalleled capacity to engage audiences on both an intellectual and emotional level. They began to recognise that the difference between whether the theatre represents a vehicle for liberation or a vehicle for oppression depends on the extent to which the audience is permitted to *participate* in and own the event. With this in mind, they began to explore devices and conventions which would change audience members from being passive spectators to active meaning makers who might affect and transform the direction, and even the content of the play itself. The manipulation of situations relating to the real lives of the participants, which is fundamental to this approach, helps them to understand that the world is not a fixed place, that the way in which our lives evolve is not inevitable, and that all situations are open to change. Boal coined the term 'Spect-actors' to represent the participants in such an experience.[1]

INTRODUCTION

◗ *Drama in Schools*

Influenced by developments in both theatre and education, the innovators of process drama desired to push the boundaries within which participants could control and manipulate the theatre event even further. In the 1980s leading practitioners such as Dorothy Heathcote and Gavin Bolton gave particular attention to devising a form of theatre which would be most appropriate to the context of the classroom. In this regard they recognised a number of needs which did not seem to be adequately addressed in traditional approaches to drama in schools. Heretofore, children had tended, for the most part, to be either audience members to a theatre event or actors in the school play. The artistic and educational benefits of these experiences were of course undeniable, in terms of familiarising children with the language and form of theatre, with developing presentational skills, and with building self-confidence. However, critical reflection on the nature of these experiences led to a re-evaluation of children's opportunities for learning not only *about*, but also learning *through* drama, within the context of education. In this regard, questions such as the following have driven experimentation in the area, particularly since the 1980s:

How can we make drama exciting, relevant, accessible and safe for all children, rather than just those who are particularly outgoing or experienced? What are the various kinds of learning that can take place during a drama encounter? Is it possible to learn about other subject areas through drama? How can the skills and knowledge related to the art form itself be best developed?

In addition to the summary given at the beginning of this introduction, it is the task of this book to explain the particular genre which emerged from these questions through theory and through practical example. Process drama is now a well-established approach to the teaching of drama in many countries. It is a testament to the many leading practitioners, innovative teachers, and children who engage with it every day, and to the nature of the approach itself, that it continues to change and evolve in innovative and exiting ways. Fundamentally, it constitutes a stimulating and challenging approach to the arts and to education generally, which we believe should be available to all children. Its introduction to the Irish primary curriculum represents an exciting departure for Irish education.

Layout of this book

The essential content of this book is based on a number of process dramas, which were facilitated and developed in primary schools throughout Ireland. For many teachers, an initial familiarity with a range of such practical examples begins to nourish an almost instinctive understanding of the principles which contribute to effective drama teaching. With this in mind, we discuss some of the earlier examples in significant practical detail. Our desire here is to provide support for, and build confidence in, the teacher who is relatively new to drama. It is not, however, to provide prescriptive lesson plans which should be followed without thought. It is important to remember that the evolution of these dramas reflected the particular contexts and desires of the children we worked with, and could easily have emerged quite differently. As the teacher progresses through the book, she will notice that the later dramas tend to be explained in terms of initial starters which are accompanied by a range of possible options. The direction which the drama might take in a particular classroom, will depend both on the responses of the children in question, and on the choices which are made with regard to the thematic and dramatic focus of the work.

So that the teacher can develop the skills to facilitate a process drama, it is most important that she understands its fundamental principles. Each drama is therefore followed by a thorough analysis of the theoretical and practical principles which underpin it. The second part of each chapter also focuses on a particular convention or approach to form, which features strongly in the preceding drama. For example, because the convention of teacher-in-role features strongly in the *Winter's Dilemma* drama for first and second class, it is followed by a thorough theoretical and practical analysis of this particular convention. Drama conventions 'are indicators of the way in which time, space and presence can interact and be imaginatively shaped to create different kinds of meanings in theatre' (Neelands, 2000, p. 4).

In this book we have given particular attention to conventions or approaches to form which we feel are fundamental, and from which we will show that a variety of other conventions are drawn.[2]

The first chapter, can be read either in advance of or after examining the various dramas of the book. This depends on the general preference of the reader in terms of when issues of philosophy and structure are most usefully consulted. In any case, the chapter should provide a helpful reference point when the teacher is planning her own dramas. The basic principles and elements of a drama experience are examined initially. We then discuss issues of progression and dramatic structure. Finally, we highlight what we have found to be fundamental skills in the practical facilitation of a drama in the classroom.

The second chapter focuses on the area of child play, from which many of the basic principles of drama teaching have evolved. It explores the notion that children bring a basic knowledge of drama elements such as role, symbol and improvisation to their early years in the primary school. The chapter explores ways in which this knowledge can be harnessed for the early years' classroom through the setting up of play areas. It then examines ways, through subtle interventions from the teacher, that children can begin to take their first steps into drama.

Chapter 3 describes a drama entitled *Winter's Dilemma*, which was devised for and with children from first and second class. From the initial stimulus of a poem entitled 'Autumn Leaves' by Irene Pawsey, we created a story about a forest in the middle of Ireland whose inhabitants are experiencing a lot of difficulty due to arguments and tensions between the seasons. Through the children's experience of this world and their attempts to reconcile its problems, they explore the themes of assertiveness and identity. The second part of the chapter focuses on the convention of teacher-in-role, the origins of which are explained in terms of both educational and theatre practice.

The drama in **Chapter 4** is based on the old Irish folktale of *The Children of Lir* and explores the themes of family, change, loyalty and jealousy. It is aimed at children from third to fifth class. The drama is designed to allow the children to explore and respond to the moments before, during and after a devastating spell is cast on the children by their stepmother. The chapter also aims to show how children can be facilitated to develop their individual capacity to express themselves and to communicate through physical image-making and creative movement. The second part of the chapter examines the theoretical and practical basis of such activity.

The stimulus for the drama in **Chapter 5** is the expedition of the famous Irish explorer Tom Crean to the Antarctic Circle in 1910 (*Terra Nova* expedition). This drama, which is aimed at children in fifth and sixth class, explores the themes of ambition, ideals and heroism. The particular focus of the second part of this chapter is on the area of improvisation and dramatic tension. While we initially discuss the notion that all drama conventions are based on the principles of improvisation, the preparation for and implementation of paired verbal improvisations is then given particular attention.

Chapter 6 focuses on using script as a stimulus for process drama. Script is also explored as a basis for writing and for performance. The content for the chapter is based on a number of adapted scenes from the screenplay *Rabbit Proof Fence* by Christine Olsen, which explores the themes of interculturalism, power and courage. Initially, we examine ways in which children can use process drama to give greater meaning to these scenes, through the building of character and context. We then discuss improvisatory approaches which support the documentation and writing of new scenes. Finally, we examine ways in which the scenes can be explored, shared and performed in an informal or formal context.

The concluding chapter highlights the wide range of theatre-related experiences which we feel should be part of the child's experience in the primary school, and which contribute powerfully to his ability to engage with process drama. This range, which is explained with examples from the Irish context, represents what is known as the drama continuum. It includes child play, process drama, theatre-in-education, children's theatre productions, and children's performances of their own work. We explore the relationship between these areas, and particularly how they contribute to the child's overall experience of process drama.

As you will note from the above, the planning of each drama is based on a different type of stimulus. The stimuli represent a range of cultural genres which the teacher can use to develop subsequent drama experiences. They include poetry, folktale, script and historical text. The material we have used in this regard is drawn from both Irish and international sources, and can be applied and adapted within a variety of contexts.

With regard to the writing conventions of the book, the teacher is referred to as 'she' throughout, and the child as 'he'. Also examples of direct speech on the part of the teacher are presented in italics.

▶ Conclusion

The writing of this book represents an exiting, creative and challenging process for its authors in terms of affirming and developing our knowledge of drama. As we continually negotiated our experience and knowledge in the schools we worked in, we discovered new things about the subjects we dealt with, the children we worked with, the form we were using, and indeed about ourselves. We hope that this aspect of discovery, which inevitably evolves from working in and through drama, will be at the heart of the teacher's engagement with this book. We hope that it will provide a launching pad for those of you who are new to the teaching of drama and additional support for those who are more experienced. In any case, we expect that the process will lead you and the children you teach into new worlds, where you will discover 'experience of a totally different order'. Enjoy the journey!

Footnotes

1　In the 1970s Augusto Boal developed a theatre form in Brazil known as forum theatre, which allowed an audience to participate and effect change in a live performance. The performance usually focuses on experiences which were derived from the collective experience of the group. It is now a popular convention which has been adapted in a wide variety of countries and within a variety of education and theatre contexts.

2 A wide range of conventions have been well documented in publications such as Neeland's *Structuring Drama Work* (1990), or Winston and Tandy's *Drama 4–11*.

Introduction

This book contains many examples of process dramas which evolved as a result of working with specific age groups in various primary schools throughout Ireland. For many teachers, an initial familiarity with a range of such examples in practice begins to nourish an instinctive understanding of the principles which contribute to effective drama experiences for children. However, it is our intention in this chapter to make these principles explicit, so that the teacher is capable of generating plans which focus on the specific needs of her own group. To this end, our intention is to provide flexible and supportive frameworks for approaching drama, while asserting the need for individual creativity, inventiveness and flexibility throughout.

It is worth reviewing at this stage the essential characteristics of process drama which were presented in the introduction to this book, and which will be developed within this chapter.

- A drama experience for children involves them entering into a fictional 'as if' situation, in order to explore relationships and themes which relate to real life.

- The purpose of using a fiction to explore such issues is both to create a safe distance for the children from the material being dealt with, and to provide a stimulating and imaginary context for their cognitive, affective and artistic exploration.

- The structure and form implicit in this process derive from the essential principles of theatre practice. As both the teacher and pupils explore and manipulate these principles throughout the process, their experience and knowledge of the art form itself is developed and extended.

- Process drama is distinct from a 'traditional' theatre performance in that it is improvisatory in nature.[1] Its outcomes are uncertain and it relies on the active emotional and intellectual engagement of all its participants for its purpose.

The aim of this chapter is to introduce teachers to the main principles involved in planning a drama experience. The conditions which we consider to be necessary for children's artistic, emotional and intellectual engagement will be highlighted, alongside those which allow them sufficient invitation and power to own, influence and transform a drama from within.

THE PLANNING PROCESS

We have divided the planning process into three main stages which reflect our experience when preparing the variety of dramas which are presented in this book.

- *Stage 1: Pre-planning Considerations*
- *Stage 2: Structuring for Dramatic Experience*
- *Stage 3: Facilitating Drama*

STAGE 1: PRE-PLANNING CONSIDERATIONS

The group	The fictional lens	The thematic focus
	• Distance • Stimulus • Roles	

Considering the Group

For many teachers who are new to teaching drama, the most daunting aspect of planning a drama is the apparently endless number of possibilities which are available for exploration. There are many possible themes and characters which can be explored, many possible conventions which can be employed and many possible ways in to the fiction. While drama is essentially an improvisatory process, some choices will have to be made in advance of the activity in order to find an effective and appropriate focus for a particular group. In this regard, there are a number of fundamental issues about the children in question which need to be considered in order to provide them with the emotional 'safety', which is required during the experience. A child's emotional safety refers to his feeling of comfort within the group and with the material to be explored, and it has a profound impact on his participation. The following issues are worth considering in terms of planning a drama which is sensitive to the particular needs of a group of children.

Social dynamic
- How well do the children in the class relate to each other?
- Are they respectful of each other's work?
- Are there children who are left out?
- Are there cliques within the class?
- Do the boys and the girls work well together?

Drama experience
- How comfortable are the children with working physically?
- How much experience do they have of working in small groups, pairs or as a whole class?
- Are there particular drama conventions which might be particularly effective given the social and artistic needs of this class?
- Which form of organisation will provide the best 'way in' for this class?

Interests and awareness

- Are there particular themes or fictional scenarios which this group might be especially interested in?

The answers to the above questions will help with the next stage of the planning process which is to match the children's needs with an appropriate fictional lens and thematic focus.[2]

Considering the Fictional Lens

▶ *Distance*

The use of a fiction in educational drama is essential to children's attraction to the process, but also to their emotional safety while they are working. Drama is an extremely powerful tool due to its holistic nature; it must therefore be facilitated with care so that children are not either manipulated during the experience or led into emotional territories which they have not agreed to.

In general, our experience is that the use of situations and contexts too close to the experience of the children tends to cause barriers to their participation. This is why we rely on the **distance** of a fiction for the context of the drama, rather than on the personal experiences of children.[3]

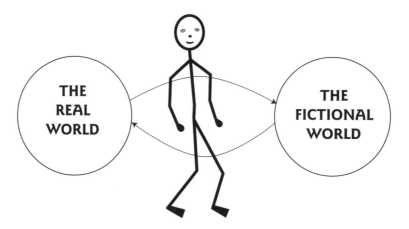

THE REAL WORLD

THE FICTIONAL WORLD

In choosing a fictional lens, the teacher can draw on a wide range of cultural stimuli including stories, poems, songs, newspaper articles, television programmes and folklore. However, her own imagination will be the most important resource a teacher has, in terms of manipulating and developing such material to suit the drama. While the children's personal experience is not replicated in the drama, it does indeed have a significant bearing on the teacher's choice of fictional lens in terms of its relevance to their lives, its capacity to respond to their interests, and to intrigue their imaginations.

- What are the children particularly interested in? Is there an aspect of the curriculum, popular culture, literature or media which has grabbed their attention recently?

- Is there a particular human theme which would be useful for this class to focus on in terms of improving the social dynamic of the group (e.g. friendship, loyalty)?

- Are there issues which are particularly sensitive for my class at the moment? Would the distance of a fictional situation help to address these, or would they be more appropriately dealt with by another person or body at another time?

The Stimulus

In this book each drama was inspired by and developed from a different type of stimulus. The *Winter's Dilemma* drama (Chapter 3) was developed from the stimulus of a poem, *The Children of Lir* drama (Chapter 4) from a folktale, the *Tom Crean* drama (Chapter 5) from a historical text, and *The Rabbit Proof Fence* drama (Chapter 6) from a script. While these were the main stimuli for planning, additional stimuli were also introduced to support the drama. Some of these were invented or manipulated by ourselves to suit the purpose of the drama. In general, effective stimuli for drama tend to include at least one of the following characteristics:

- An existing tension
- An unanswered question
- An invitation to get involved
- A sense of intrigue
- A sense of authenticity
- The potential to build belief
- The potential for thematic exploration

▶ Stories

Folktales, fairytales, myths, local folklore, contemporary literature, 'made up' stories, or stories within songs can provide exciting and engaging starting points for a drama. Stories have the advantage of containing a basic plot, themes and a set of characters to improvise with. However, it is important that participants are not tied to a linear representation of the original plot. The notion of expanding the exploration to include moments, before, during and after the original story can release teachers and children from reproduction into a more meaningful, imaginative and thematic exploration.

▶ Documents

The effect of information emerging in the form of an official document can often add more excitement, urgency and authenticity to a drama than a verbal statement by the teacher. Documents associated with *public* life can include passports, tickets, birth and death certificates, announcements, decrees, posters, notices, photographs, newspaper articles, AGM reports, schools reports and maps. Such documents can herald an imminent arrival, an unexpected change in date for a certain event, an affirmation (or not) of an identity, evidence of a journey having been taken, a festival or commemoration to be prepared for and so on.

Documents associated with a character's *private* life include letters, diaries, half-written notes, cards (birthday, sympathy, wedding, christening), photographs and drawings. These documents can also launch and progress the action of a drama, but they have the special effect of inviting a more intimate exploration of character, as they invite us to consider the private thoughts, feelings and relationships of a particular individual. These documents can be tantalisingly incomplete and therefore can provide opportunities for further dramatic exploration.

▶ *Artefacts*

The careful manipulation of artefacts and objects during a drama experience can be particularly effective in terms of providing the authenticity and intrigue which is necessary to the children's engagement. Almost any object can be made valuable, invaluable, special or frightening depending on the way in which it is treated by the teacher or the participants. Objects or artefacts associated with *public* life include historical artefacts from or for a museum, artefacts associated with important rituals in a community or tribe (e.g. a crown, a sword for a knighting ceremony, weapons belonging to or passed down from inspirational leaders, ceremonial robes), jewellery, masks and architectural models.

Objects or artefacts associated with a character's *private* life can include items which are the private property of an individual and are sometimes saved for a particular reason e.g. jewellery, precious stones, clothing, objects associated with a particular hobby (e.g. paintbrush, football jersey, musical instruments), books, CDs, videos and photographs. The container or location for a set of personal objects can have a significant impact on the meaning which is drawn from them e.g. an old dusty shoe box found in an attic, a sports bag found at a bus stop, or an ornate jewellery box found in a castle.

▶ *Photographs and Paintings*

Photographs and paintings can provide a variety of functions in a drama experience. Firstly they can very effectively provide a sense of time and place. Photographs can also provide vital background information or raise important questions in a very efficient and indirect manner. Consider the impact of a photograph of a group of passengers lining up for the *Titanic* in this regard. They can also be used in terms of compiling evidence, and bringing a sense of authenticity to a situation. Such material might be sought from a personal store, photography shops, art galleries or the internet.

▶ *Theatrical Props and Media*

Props and supports associated with presentational forms of theatre are also used in process drama to explore, express and represent meaning. For example, the use of simple lighting and music can help to transport children into another world, or heighten and give focus to work which has already been prepared.

Scarves, fabric and clothes from a distant era or context can be used to build character and context. (Note the use of fabric to create landscape in *Winter's Dilemma* and *The Children of Lir*.) The use of masks and puppets in a drama can challenge children to explore and develop characters beyond the naturalistic genre. In general, theatrical props and media not only help to create atmosphere and support the aesthetic and emotional quality of the drama, but can also provide provocative media for exploration of both character and situation.

Roles

> *Metaxis – The state of belonging completely and simultaneously to two different autonomous worlds: the image of reality and the reality of the image . . .'*
>
> (Boal, 1995, p. 42)

A powerful feature of dramatic activity is that of approaching a fictional context in role. As you will observe from the dramas in this book, the children tend to approach the material through a variety of roles such as villagers, explorers, interviewers, museum workers and so on. Working in role allows the child to view the world from a particular and often new perspective. The learning which accrues from such activity takes place at various levels. For example, at the early stages of the *Tom Crean* drama, the child tends to consciously create the explorer as 'type' and learns about the skills, tasks and viewpoint of an arctic explorer. As the drama progresses, he engages experientially with the facts, details and tensions of Tom Crean's experience, and he moves from a more conscious construction of generic role (i.e. an explorer) to a more holistic engagement with a particular character and his dilemma. When the child as Tom Crean is unexpectedly asked to leave the expedition, he explores his response to the human dilemma of being asked to give up something which one has invested in very deeply. In this drama the child uses his previous knowledge to create the fictional role, and learns new things about himself and the wider world within the fiction itself.

▶ Choosing Roles

> *I take it as a general rule that people have most power to become involved at a caring and urgently involved level if they are placed in a quite specific relationship with the action, because this brings with it inevitably the responsibility, and more particularly, the viewpoint, which gets them into effective involvement.*
>
> (Heathcote, 1984, p. 168)

Role is not only employed for its educational and artistic benefits but also for its unparalleled capacity to engage and motivate children. However, as Heathcote points out above, the level and type of engagement achieved is based to a large extent on the creation of an appropriate match between the children's role and the material in question. For example, the main role which was chosen for the children in *Winter's Dilemma* was the inhabitants of the forest. This was because the inhabitants of the forest would be most affected by a potential disturbance in the seasons.[4] When choosing roles for or with the children, it is important to consider the *need* which a particular fictional group has, to know, care about or challenge something within a given situation.

In the *Tom Crean* drama the children were given the responsibility of being museum curators who had the task of researching and creating a monument to Tom Crean's life. Putting the children into official positions of responsibility in relation to the chosen subject matter is another way of creating a need to be involved. The following are examples of various types of roles which we have found particularly effective in engaging children's commitment within a drama.

- Roles that assume a high level responsibility e.g. jury, government ministries, business enterprises, police, event managers, tour operators, groups of spiritual or tribal leaders.

- Roles that investigate and record e.g. journalists, interviewers, historians, archaeologists, policemen and women, government agencies, employees of museums, travel agencies or artists.

- Roles that function to support a particular community e.g. a community living at the edge of a forest might include lumberjacks, carpenters, shopkeepers, environmental groups, tour operators, festival organisers, teachers, priests, builders or parents.

You may notice that many of the above roles are particularly conducive to working with a large group. When children are given a collective identity and purpose in the fiction, it has the effect of increasing their levels of co-operation and motivation, particularly in the early stages. However, while they are necessarily bound together by a common interest, they are not precluded from developing a variety of individual roles within a grouping, nor are they precluded from having a variety of individual opinions on an issue. For example, in the *Winter's Dilemma* drama, while the inhabitants of the forest are bound together by a common interest in rectifying the seasonal irregularities, they may adopt a variety of individual roles within such a community (e.g. lumberjacks, shopkeepers), and have a variety of opinions about how the problem should be addressed.

In some dramas it may be appropriate for the children to personalise their roles even further. For example, after the initial context-building stages within a drama about homelessness, the children might create profiles to represent a variety of individuals who might find themselves in such situations. In these profiles a child can identify a particular background for a character/individual such as his/her age, hometown, education and previous employment. Such background can provide for depth and commitment during subsequent exploration (e.g. interviews in pairs, still images of moments of choice). In our discussion of Stage 3: Structuring for Dramatic Experience, we will focus more specifically on how we can help children to develop belief and investment in their roles within the early context-building stage of the drama.

Considering the Thematic Focus

▶ *Themes and Underlying Questions*

Due to the necessary collaboration between teacher and children in a drama, many of the learning and artistic objectives tend to emerge within the process itself. However, it is important to balance the open-ended nature of the process with the need for focus. *What themes are we trying to explore? What underlying questions are we asking through this work?* In the planning of any drama some reflection on the above questions will be essential. Some of the themes explored in the dramas of this book include friendship, family, jealousy, interculturalism, power and loyalty.

In general, it is important for the teacher to be clear about the area of human enquiry the children are being asked to focus on, without dictating their actual response to it. In this regard we have found it useful to identify one or two philosophical or underlying questions which are provocative enough to encourage a variety of avenues for exploration. For example, the underlying question in a drama exploring leadership might include: *What does it mean to be a good leader? How do we choose our leaders?* Obviously these questions are not asked directly of the children, but are explored indirectly through the overall *experience* of the drama. The diagram below illustrates the initial brainstorm which led to the identification of a thematic focus for *Winter's Dilemma*. Clearly the teacher's decisions in this regard will be influenced by the needs of the particular group in question.

STIMULUS	BRAINSTORM OF ALL POSSIBLE THEMES	THEMATIC FOCUS	UNDERLYING QUESTIONS
Winter's Dilemma	*Power* *Dealing with bullies* *Change* *Revenge* *The seasons* *Being special*	• Being special • Assertiveness/ bullying	• What makes us special? • How do we respond to people who treat us badly?

Examples of underlying questions from the dramas of this book

Drama	Underlying questions
• *Winter's Dilemma* (Ch. 3)	• What makes us special? How do we respond to people who treat us badly?
• *The Children of Lir* (Ch. 4)	• How do we respond to change? What impact does jealousy have on relationships?
• *The Explorations of Tom Crean* (Ch. 5)	• How do we reconcile our dreams and ambitions with our reality? What does it mean to be a hero?

STAGE 2: STRUCTURING FOR DRAMATIC EXPERIENCE

The dramatist must draw the audience as soon as possible into a state of intense concern with the event while at the same time building the dramatic world. The leader or drama teacher working in process drama has exactly the same task to accomplish.

(O'Neill, 1995, p. 455)

▶ *The Drama Teacher and the Playwright*

Cecily O'Neill draws our attention above to the similarity in function between the playwright or dramatist, and the teacher in process drama. In order to draw the children into a state of 'intense concern' with the event, the teacher needs to learn to understand and manipulate the elements of theatre, not only before the drama begins, as the playwright does, but also in negotiation with the children within the drama experience itself. This requires the consideration of engaging contexts, characters and pre-texts to initially draw the children in, while providing real opportunities for improvisation and transformation throughout.

While it is impossible and undesirable to provide a generic blueprint for drama lessons, we attempt in this section to use the general stages which tend to be common to both 'play making' and process drama to help the teacher to begin to initiate her own classroom dramas. To this end, we will try to review the elements which have been considered in the pre-planning stage (group, fictional lens, dramatic focus), in terms of how they may be translated into practice to engage children in the 'now time' of drama.

◗ *Scenes and Moments*

> *For any drama, no matter what her goal, Heathcote's plan is to work slowly, to take time for the class to become committed and for belief to be built. This does not mean she stands still or repeats work. Instead, she thinks of as many different ways as she can to stay in the same place while seeming to move forward.*
>
> (Wagner, 1979, p. 112)

Like the playwright, the teacher and the children will be approaching drama in terms of scenes or moments, rather than in terms of a linear plot line. This is based on the notion that complex issues such as character motivation, relationship, theme and representation are better addressed by slowing down the action and 'digging deeper' into particular sections. As we become less concerned with what *happens* next, our excavations tend to be guided by what moments we *need* to look at next, or who we *need* to meet next, in order to understand the situation better or to examine it from a different angle. In this regard, participants may wish to move between the present, past and future in their explorations.

In contrast with a scene in a traditional play, which is scripted and rehearsed, the moment in a process drama is explored spontaneously without a script. However the teacher, and indeed the participants, will almost always need to consider at least some of the following questions before a particular moment can be explored through improvisation.

- *Who* is involved? (Role)
- *Where* is it happening? (Place)
- *When* is it happening? (Time)
- *What* is provoking the action? (Tension)
- How might the moment address the thematic focus? (Theme)
- What dramatic convention will best amplify this moment e.g. teacher-in-role, paired improvisation? (Convention)

It should also be remembered that in process drama, moments can be explored either as a whole class, in small groups, in pairs, or individually, depending on the dramatic convention being used or the social needs of the class at a particular time.

▶ *Choosing Moments in a Drama Experience*

In terms of choosing moments in a drama, and considering the order in which they might be explored, the general issues which effect progression in both a theatre play and in a process drama will now be discussed.

As has been stated previously, one of the biggest challenges for the teacher and the children in process drama resides in the fact that planning takes place not only in advance of the journey but also during the journey itself. This is why a more general understanding of the structural factors which have been found to impact on both genres will be particularly helpful.

Let us first consider the dual focus of any drama experience in terms of the teacher's role. As the diagram below suggests the teacher needs to be conscious of both *levels of engagement* and opportunities for *thematic exploration* at all times throughout the process. These aspects are interwoven in complex ways throughout the drama but stated simply, the teacher has little hope of engaging the children with the underlying thematic questions discussed earlier, if they are not sufficiently engaged or intrigued in the first place.

Progression in a drama experience[5]

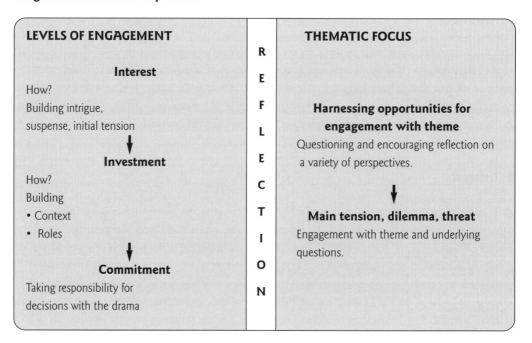

In the next section we will use the diagram above to explore how moments and tasks might be chosen by the group throughout the process, so that children will be adequately motivated to 'care' when more complex challenges related to theme begin to emerge.

Levels of Engagement – Building Belief

▶ *Contract*

In general, the effect of the drama contract is to clarify the 'rules of the game' in a variety of respects, so that all participants have an understanding of the nature of the work, and of what is expected of them during the process. Children who are unfamiliar with drama should learn through direct discussion and through experience that they will need to accept responsibility for the direction of the drama. It should be understood that all individual contributions should be respected, while accepting that some decisions will need to be negotiated as a group.

Just as the acceptance of a fictional reality in the theatre is not possible without the collusion of the audience, neither is the plausibility of a process drama without an agreement on the part of its participants to *believe*. The following is an example of contract making from the *Winter's Dilemma* drama:

As you suggested yesterday, our drama is going to take place in a forest, do you think we could 'be' the type of people or animals who could live in a forest? Do you think we could all believe that for a little while?

One of the important things to note about the contract above is the acknowledgement that what is about to happen is not real, and that we are 'making it happen'. Paradoxically, as a result of this acknowledgement of pretence, children tend subsequently to feel more liberty to believe in the fiction. They also tend to feel less compelled to check for the factual 'truth' of every new piece of information or evidence that is given to them in the drama. The question of whether the teacher is 'making things up', which may have been a concern otherwise, now becomes irrelevant.

▶ *Interest*

As in all theatrical and educational endeavours, the main aim of the first few minutes of the drama is to capture the imaginations of the children – to intrigue, to invite and to 'hook' them into the fiction. The teacher can employ many strategies to try to ensure this initial engagement. For example, the introduction to a drama often involves some form of information which is incomplete in some way, and which holds an initial tension or unanswered question. It also tends to imply a very tentative suggestion that help or action of some kind may be needed. In the 'Pre-planning Considerations' section, various stimuli were discussed in terms of both initiating and supporting a drama experience. The teacher can manipulate such stimuli, or a teacher-in-role encounter, to effectively initiate tension at the beginning of a drama e.g. a half-written diary, a letter of request, a story with a problem, a character who needs help, an artefact or group of objects that need examining. Early signs of willingness to engage or offer contributions to this initial 'offering', which is sometimes referred to as the pretext for the drama, should be welcomed and validated with sincerity by the teacher.

◗ *Investment*

The children's initial agreement to become involved, along with their general curiosity about the situation paves the way for the important task of collaboratively building the context of the drama. This generally involves moments and tasks which will create a more concrete sense of the people, time and place of the drama. At this point we are already moving away from merely talking *about* the drama in a hypothetical way, to engaging with it in a more physical, tangible and experiential form. The two main areas which will help to address this need in a drama are those of identifying and building *roles*, and creating a more concrete sense of *place*.

Investment in role

If, as previously discussed, one of the main aims of drama is to allow children to engage with a variety of perspectives while in role, a significant amount of attention needs to be given to building belief and investment in the role in question. As you will observe from the following diagram, we have found that attention to specific experiential tasks and moments while in role, yields a high level of investment. For example, in order for the children to adequately identify themselves with the role of explorer in the Tom Crean drama (Chapter 5), they physically engage with a variety of tasks which would be integral to such a role, e.g. dressing appropriately for the expedition, preparing the vehicles and packing for the journey.

The examples of possible moments for exploration in the left column below could be applicable to the development of a wide variety of roles. In terms of providing a form through which these moments can be explored, the column on the right lists a range of conventions which could be applied to each one. The choice of convention or task in each case will depend on the nature of the moment in question, the particular stage of the drama, the drama experience of the children, and the social dynamic of the group at a particular point in the lesson. These and other drama conventions will be discussed in more detail within the remaining chapters of the book.

MOMENTS/POSSIBILITIES	CONVENTIONS/TASKS
• A day in the life of an individual or group • Memories from the past • Hopes and ambitions for the future • Objects/artefacts associated with an individual or group • Significant events or signs of tension	• Mime • Still images: photographs, monuments • Interviews for newspaper, agency, history book • Hot seating, teacher-in-role: leaders, characters, significant individuals • Paper placement • Role on the wall • Diaries, journals, newspaper articles: created or found

Investment in place

As is the case when watching a play in the theatre, our awareness of the place in which action occurs affects our understanding of the situation. For example, despite its similar content, a conversation which takes place in a kitchen will be very different from a conversation which takes place at the back of a courtroom. In process drama, attention to place in concrete terms assists children in their belief in the drama, and in their engagement with role. For example, in the *Winter's Dilemma* drama (Chapter 3), the children create Winter's den before they meet him for the first time. They do this by improvising with the classroom furniture, and by using paper placement to represent the items and objects in Winter's den, which gives greater insight to his character. The following diagram provides suggestions which will help to enhance children's awareness of place within a particular drama.

MOMENTS/POSSIBILITIES	TASKS
Significant places	**To create, examine or complete**
• Bedroom	• Maps
• Town, village	• Architectural drawings
• Significant building	• Sound collage
• Park	• Paper placement
• Country, island	• Arrangement of furniture
• Hideout, den	• Use of symbols, props

◗ *Narrative and Poetic Action*

The acknowledgement by Jonothan Neelands of different types of action in drama, is helpful in terms of both naming what we do, and bringing our attention to the variety of modes within the theatre art form, which children should have an opportunity to explore, and which enhance their engagement with meaning (Neelands, 1990). While he identifies four types of action – context-building action, narrative action, poetic action and reflective action – we would like to focus specifically at this point on the notion that a teacher's awareness of both narrative and poetic action during the investment stage of a drama, has a significant impact on the aesthetic and emotional quality of the work.

Narrative action refers to action which tends to move the drama on and which allows children to explore new dimensions of plot which had not previously been considered e.g. the development of new moments on the journey to Winter's den in the *Winter's Dilemma* drama. During such activity, the children are beginning to own the drama and take responsibility for its direction. Poetic action emphasises action which allows children to explore the effect of representation and form on meaning. Engagement with symbol and image will be a strong feature of poetic action e.g. the children create Aoife's spell through movement and choral representation in *The Children of Lir* drama. They also explore the transformation of the children into swans through dance. As you may discern from these examples, most moments in drama tend to combine both types of action to a greater or lesser extent.

▶ Commitment

The goal of any drama experience is that motivation is raised to such a level that children find themselves willingly taking responsibility for important decisions, and that the teacher's primary role is that of facilitator to the process. As alluded to earlier, there is a certain point at which this willingness becomes an imperative need or emotional concern for the children which leads them to action. Dramatic tension is at the heart of this transition.

In terms of creating the conditions for such development, the teacher should be conscious of the ways in which *tension* can be gradually built throughout the drama. In the initial stages, this tension might take the form of a need to hide, to escape, to help or to do something within a limited period of time. However, in the later stages, a larger tension needs to be inserted which threatens the equilibrium of the drama and which relies on the children's investment in the context and in their roles to do so. This larger tension might take the form of a threat, a difficult dilemma, a challenging decision, or a double-edged opportunity. These larger tensions are carefully chosen by the teacher not only to increase commitment, but very importantly to bring the themes and underlying questions of the drama into direct focus.

Commitment, theme and dramatic tension

Drama	Underlying question	Threat/challenge	Means of introducing threat, challenge	Moments/tasks – attempted resolution
Winter's Dilemma (first/ second class)	How do we deal with those who treat us badly?	That Winter will not be let back into the forest; that there will only be three seasons.	Signs around the forest – 'Let's keep Winter out of the forest'.	Seeking help from the Queen of the Forest. Confrontation between Winter and Summer.
Tom Crean (fifth/ sixth class)	How do we reconcile our dreams and ambitions with our reality?	Tom is asked to return home from the expedition.	Child briefed as Captain Scott to inform Tom of his dismissal.	Children respond as Tom during meeting with Captain Scott.
	What does it mean to be a hero?	How will Tom be remembered?	A request from head of museum to provide monument/ memorial to Tom Crean.	Activities, conventions undertaken to create a memorial to Tom Crean.

▶ *Reflection*

Drama is both an experiential and reflective art form. By its nature it has the tendency to complicate and challenge easy answers to life issues. One of the most important aims of drama is that children would begin to become aware of the complexity of a given situation as a result of exploring it from various angles. They are not required to entirely 'solve' or agree on all issues during the encounter itself, but to become aware of its inherent tensions and possibilities.

Reflection can take place both during and after a drama experience and can be initiated through questioning and discussion, or through further artistic and experiential engagement. The teacher will be led both by the thematic focus of the drama and the interests of the children, in terms of the level and nature of reflection required at a particular stage in the drama.

STAGE 3: FACILITATING DRAMA

> *I like to imagine these guides, the liminal servants to the work, trying to lead the way while walking backward, so that they do not become intent on reaching a predetermined destination as quickly as possible. It is as important for these guides to know the traveller's starting point, and the nature of the journey so far, as it is to determine the kind of journey that lies ahead. In process drama, the outcome of the journey is the journey itself. The experience is its own destination.*
>
> (O'Neill, 1995, p. 67)

Facilitation, which refers to the way in which the teacher relates to the children during the drama itself, is the third stage of the planning process. We have included it as part of the planning process because the children must have the power to own and impact upon all moments and decisions within the process itself in order to glean any benefits from the experience. In this regard the teacher, as O'Neill suggests, is like a 'guide' or 'liminal servant' to the work, as the initial framework for the process is gradually handed over to and transformed by the children. In our experience, the best way to begin to acquire the skills implicit in such a role is to try to gain as much experience of teaching drama as possible, which at certain times involves taking comfortable risks and at other times a leap of faith!

The second part of each chapter in this book gives specific guidance in relation to the implementation of a range of dramatic conventions. However, the following skills will be central to most dramatic activity:

- *Working as dramatist*: While the teacher's function was compared with that of a playwright in the earlier stages of planning, she takes the wider role of dramatist within the process itself. In other words, she employs her growing knowledge of dramatic form, structure and sign, to respond to the evolving process. The combination of this knowledge in practice and her own creative and imaginative instincts will allow her to work as a teacher and as an artist simultaneously.

- *Demonstrating belief*: Whether the teacher is initiating the pre-text for a drama, working in teacher-in-role or responding to suggestions, the children's belief in the drama will always be linked to the level of seriousness with which the teacher approaches the work.

- *Validating and challenging*: Drama is an exciting but sometimes daunting experience for children, particularly those who are new to such a process. Every effort should be made to acknowledge and validate their engagement with the art form whether in or out of role. This is particularly important at the early stages of a drama, or when working with children who are less familiar with drama.

- *Observing and responding*: With regard to maintaining a balance between the initial plan and the subsequent input of the children, the teacher's most important skills are those of careful, critical and active listening and watching. Such focused observation will centre on the areas of engagement, safety, comfort with the art form and belief. It will assist the teacher in reflecting back the children's ideas to them, so that they can see more clearly their options for progression.

- *Encouraging maximum participation*: The teacher should make every effort to gain the participation of all children in the group. The use of simultaneous paired and small group activity can be very helpful in this regard, particularly in terms of enlisting the participation of shyer children. Participation is increased when children realise that in drama, contributions are made in a voluntary rather than forced capacity. Throughout the book we also discuss the many indirect ways in which participation can be increased through the teacher's use of dramatic tension.

Footnotes

1 A traditional theatre performance here refers to a performance which tends to separate actors and audience using conventions which confine the role of the audience member to that of a spectator. However, as suggested in the introduction, modern theatre practice also includes more participative approaches which tend towards much of the philosophy and some of the conventions of process drama.

2 The term 'fictional lens' which is used in the new drama curriculum for Irish primary schools is one which we have found particularly helpful. (*Teacher Guidelines*, 1999, p. 41).

3 Brian Edmunston (Ohio State University, USA) and Luke Abbott (Essex Local Education Authority, UK) used this framework to discuss 'metaxis' at an ADEI workshop in St Patrick's College, Dublin (20 January 2001). We have found it very helpful.

4 Some groups or issues may require the use of a role which, while involving a social or professional need to invest in the situation, allows the children more emotional distance from its content. This of course will depend on the particular personal experiences of a group of children. For example, in a drama which explores the themes of separation and loss, the teacher may enrol her group as social workers researching a village that has been rumoured to have lost its laughter. They might subsequently hot seat the teacher in a variety of specifically chosen roles, rather than become the roles themselves.

5 The left column represents an adaptation and development of Dorothy Heathcote's description of levels of student involvement during a drama experience.

Chapter 2
DRAMA AND PLAY IN THE EARLY YEARS

(Junior and Senior Infants)

What Is Play?

This chapter will focus on the nature of children's play and provide teachers or carers with ways of approaching play in the classroom environment. Play is a key method through which children of early years access knowledge about the world they live in. It is a natural activity which children, especially in the age range two to six years, freely engage in throughout their lives. When children play they move into the 'what if' world both physically and emotionally, a world where time and space are transformed into a different reality. In this world they adopt new identities and play with 'ideas and characteristics of their culture and environment' (Hendy and Toon, 2001, p. 3).

Play acts as a powerful context for learning and development; it is the medium through which children make sense of the world.

A long established belief that play is central to learning can be drawn from the philosophies of Rousseau, Froebel, Montessori and Isaacs. More recently the value of play was examined by Piaget (1962), Bruner (1996), Vygotsky (1978), Singer and Singer (1990) and Smilansky (1990). They all claim that play develops children socially, emotionally, affectively, cognitively and culturally. Vygotsky further advanced the idea that 'in play, a child behaves beyond his average age, above his daily behaviour; in play it is as though he were a head taller than himself' (Vygotsky, 1978, p. 102). This 'growth' takes place during play as children become 'problem setters, problem solvers and decision makers' (Hendy and Toon, 2001, p. 61). Language is developed as children think through and negotiate meaning about the world.

Free play: children-in-role as parents

▶ Characteristics of Play

The creation of a fictional world by children relies on children's perception of the world for its content. Children create and engage with this world by unconsciously employing drama elements such as belief, role, place, time and symbol.

Play emerged after two children watched their parents prepare for a birthday party. Once the party was finished the children set about mimicking their parents' actions; they became their parents (role) in an effort to explore what it might be like to behave as they did. The garden was set up by the children as the kitchen and entertainment area (dramatic place). In role as the parents, the children cooked and organised the 'treats' and spoke about the games the 'visitors' would play at the party; they interacted with the 'imaginary' visitors when they arrived. This type of play is termed socio-dramatic play. Socio-dramatic play describes the kind of play children engage in when they mimic real life interactions.

This example of the children preparing for a birthday party demonstrated the application of these elements; children worked towards building belief in their roles and in the fictional situation of the birthday party (time). The garden was set up to depict the kitchen and dining area (dramatic place). Objects were used in a symbolic way to portray this place: a chair became a table, cereal boxes represented chairs for the imaginary guests, and a chair represented the pirate ship which would be used for the party game. In addition, as the children played they seemed to employ their own implicit set of behavioural rules associated with operating in the fictional situation. They understood the importance of believing in the fictional world they were in the process of creating.

▶ Rationale for Teacher Intervention in Play

The example of children creating the world of the birthday party demonstrates the natural way play can be initiated by children. Children had ample space and resources to inhabit the fictional world spontaneously in their home environment. Free play is the term used to describe the spontaneous way children inhabit and develop the fictional world uninterrupted by an adult. In the classroom context, it can happen that children may not be able to engage as spontaneously with play. Lack of space, increasing class numbers and timetable restrictions can place limitations on children. Therefore the teacher may need to assist in either helping to initiate children's play or spotting possibilities for intervention once the children have initiated their own play.

The benefits of effective teacher intervention in children's learning are well documented in the literature. Vygotsky (1978) emphasised that adults can move a child from his current level of development to a more sophisticated level of understanding through a process called 'scaffolding'. He refers to this as 'the zone of proximal development (ZPD), the distance between the actual level of development as determined by the child's existing ability at problem solving, and the level of potential development under adult guidance' (Vygotsky, 1978).

Many theories have been suggested about the different ways a teacher can intervene to harness the inherent learning possibilities of a developing play situation. These theories apply if the teacher decides to initiate children's play, or if the teacher decides to intervene once children have initiated their own play. Gura (2002) believes that optimal learning can take place if the teacher and the child become partners in play. Sayeed and Guerin (2000) advocate that teacher intervention should be a mediated learning experience (MLE). Cairney (1991) uses the term 'information giver', meaning sharer, interested listener, opinion sharer, introducer, demonstrator and critical fellow learner, to describe what should happen when the teacher intervenes in children's play. We would argue that the teacher would interchange between all of these roles when she is seeking to support and develop children's learning.

▶ Ways of Approaching Teacher Intervention

It has already been highlighted that children's play may not emerge naturally in a classroom environment given the constraints which can exist. As a result, a teacher may choose to either initiate children's play or intervene while children are playing. The following section will outline approaches which can be taken in this regard. Different intervention approaches will be explained using a play based on space exploration. The context of space exploration can be described as fantasy play. Fantasy play is the term used to describe a play in which the situation and some of the characters chosen do not parallel with the real world e.g. children may inhabit Mars and become aliens! Fantasy contexts offer children emotional safety, as they are one step removed from reality.

Whether a teacher chooses to initiate children's play or intervene while children are playing, it must be remembered that a teacher should never attempt to lead or control children's efforts. Children need to feel that it is their play and that they have ownership of it. This is essential, as the quality of children's commitment to the fictional world will affect their imaginative, physical and emotional engagement. An over directed and prescriptive approach will inhibit children from engaging in the imaginative world and will consequently hinder their learning. With this in mind, the teacher will be seeking to balance the support offered with children's freedom to create the imaginary world for themselves.

▶ Before Play: Initiating Children's Play

A teacher will often choose to initiate children into the fictional world if they have not been accustomed to using play in the classroom before. This process can either involve deciding the fictional world for the children or inviting children to suggest a fictional world for themselves. A question such as *I wonder what imaginative place you would like to visit today?* opens up possibilities for the children to decide on their own world. Alternatively, asking children, *I wonder what would it be like to go into space?* identifies the world for the children at the outset. Once the fictional world has been decided, discussion can then be used to help children to reflect on who might inhabit the world, where the world will be located and how it might be represented.

Discussing potential roles (who)
- What is the name of people that go into space?
- How will the crew prepare for a space trip? What kind of things might need to be done beforehand?
- What kind of jobs/responsibilities might people have while on board?
- What will they eat?
- If they reach a planet, will there be life on the planet?
- Who will live there?
- What might those who live there do everyday?

Imagining the place (where)
- How will we get up to space?
- Where should the rocket take off? (A teacher can point to various parts of the play area.)
- How will we create the space rocket? What could we use? Do you have any suitable materials which you could bring in from home?
- What interesting places might the space rocket visit?
- How will we create these places?

Resources

Bringing in personal resources from home to furnish the play world will assist children in gaining ownership of this world. In addition, a variety of props such as puppets, telephones, dolls, balls, clay, play dough, magic dust, boxes or blocks can be supplied by the teacher. It is a good idea to encourage children to use props in a symbolic or realistic way e.g. chairs and brushes could be used to create the space rocket. Magic dust might be used for take-off! When choosing props consideration needs to be given to issues such as diversity and gender. Therefore, an array of toys with different skin tones should be chosen along with ensuring that girls and boys have an assortment of toys available to them. In addition, religious beliefs also need to be considered when choosing dolls, as dolls are not permitted in some cultures (Moyles 1994).

▶ *Free Play*

Once the teacher has helped children to initiate play, ample time will then need to be given to them to inhabit the fictional world and to develop the fictional roles for themselves. Free play is the term used to describe the period when children gain ownership of their play world.

Free play: creating the space rocket

Free play: negotiating the finer details before take-off

▶ *Teacher Intervention during Play*

The next section focuses on ways in which a teacher might intervene if children have initiated a play about space exploration. Smilansky (1968) advocates two methods of teacher intervention which can be adopted during children's play. He refers to these methods as outside and inside intervention.

Outside intervention involves the teacher asking questions or making comments about what is happening in children's play once the play has already started. To the child these comments should appear incidental in nature, but the teacher will be using them to probe and develop children's learning.

Inside intervention involves developing the learning potential of the play by entering the children's fictional world in role (teacher–in–role). Attention will now be drawn to the principles underlying teacher intervention before discussing outside and inside intervention.

Successful intervention depends on a teacher understanding how and when to intervene, as intervening too soon and cutting children's play short can damage the fragile play process. Therefore, time spent observing children free playing with imaginary roles and situations will pay dividends later. This time will give the teacher an opportunity to understand the fictional world the child is in the process of creating. It also enables the teacher to gain some insight into the child's perspective of this world. This understanding will help the teacher accept, respect and believe in the children's fictional world, and as a result the teacher will be in a better position to harness the inherent learning opportunities of the situation. The observation period can also be used to evaluate children's social competences (communication and co-operation skills) and their ability to work in role.

▶ Outside Intervention

Outside intervention can be achieved by asking questions and making comments about characters and situations which exist in the children's play world. It is best if the teacher addresses the children-in-role. All responses should be treated with authenticity before being further probed. Definitive right and wrong answers should not be sought. Questions which could be asked of children's play about space exploration will now be examined. Examples of questions which seek to probe, challenge and develop children's problem-solving capacity will be provided.

Initial questions
- *This looks very interesting . . . I wonder could you tell me a little about what is happening?*
- *I have never been in a space rocket before; I would love to know more about the way it works.*

Probing questions
- *Will it be safe in space?*
- *How do you manage to eat when in space?*
- *Have you encountered any difficulties so far?*

Adding complexity
- *How long have you been working in this area?*
- *What did you have to think of in advance of departure?*
- *How long will you be in space?*
- *What kind of food will you bring with you?*
- *How will you keep it fresh?*
- *Will you all have specific jobs to attend to in space?*
- *What will happen if a fight develops between the astronauts on board?*

Theme exploration: difference
- *Are there any notable differences between the aliens and yourselves?*
- *Do you think there is anything the astronauts can learn from these aliens?*
- *Can they learn anything from you?*
- *What should you do when you meet new people?*

The following table provides helpful categories for deciding on questions and illustrates open questions.

Summary guideline (outside intervention)

PURPOSE OF QUESTION	EXAMPLE OF QUESTION
• Elicit information	• Can you tell me about . . . ?
• Supply information	• Did you know that . . . ?
• Build identification with place and role	• How long have you been working as . . . ? • What is your job like?
• Insert tension	• How might you deal with . . . ? • How would you feel if . . . ? • What would happen if . . . ?
• Deepen initial response	• Tell me a little more about . . . • What do you need in order to . . . ?

▶ Inside Intervention (Teacher-in-role)

Inside intervention is another approach which can be employed by the teacher once children have commenced playing. As already mentioned, this involves the teacher interacting in role in the children's fiction (teacher-in-role). From this standpoint, the teacher can respond and structure the learning from 'within'. She can insert complexities and challenges for the children to respond to (see Chapter 3 dealing with teacher-in-role). A number of roles are available for the teacher to choose from.

▶ Types of Roles

The teacher tends to adopt a high status or a low status role during her interaction with the children in play.

▶ High Status Role

The teacher could enter a space play as an inspector examining health and safety issues relating to the rocket before departure. Further tensions can be added when children are comfortable communicating with the teacher in this way. The teacher could suggest the possibility of closure if they cannot explain clearly the various safety measures which were taken by the team. It is important to validate all responses.

ROLE	PLAY CONTEXT	TEACHER INPUT	LEARNING OBJECTIVES
Captain of space shuttle	Space Rocket	• I am the captain of this spacecraft, I believe you want to come with me to space, tell me what you can offer us?	Interview skills, assertiveness
Health and safety officer	Restaurant	• How do you make sure that this restaurant is free from any germs? This is very important as I will have to close the restaurant if I notice any problems.	Understanding personal hygiene
Character complaining	Shop	• I want to complain about this sandwich, it appears to have a very unusual smell. I am very surprised as everything is usually perfect.	Dealing with complaints

▶ Low Status Role

A lower status role helps to validate children and put them in an expert role. In such a situation the teacher becomes a character who needs assistance from the children. In the space rocket example the teacher could become a person about to apply to become an astronaut. As a result, she needs to draw on the children's expertise in this area.

Examples of roles and other drama contexts which could be developed will be outlined in the following table. The context of a space station, a restaurant, a shop and a doctor's surgery will be used for this purpose.

ROLE	PLAY CONTEXT	TEACHER INPUT	LEARNING OBJECTIVES
Character in need of help	Space Rocket	• I'm really scared that we have forgotten something, are you sure we made adequate preparation for this journey? What did you bring to eat? Tell me what other things you brought with you?	Preparing for journeys
Character in need of help	Restaurant	• I need to book my wedding hotel. What can you offer me? What is your menu like? I want it to be a very special day and will really need your help.	Organisational skills Sales skills
Character in need of help	Shop	• I need to purchase a healthy lunch for my children; they are going on a school tour. I heard you have some interesting items in stock, can you help me please?	Healthy eating
Character in need of help	Doctor's surgery	• I'm the secretary and I notice that people come into this surgery very worried. What should I say to put them at their ease?	Health care

Summary of high status and low status roles

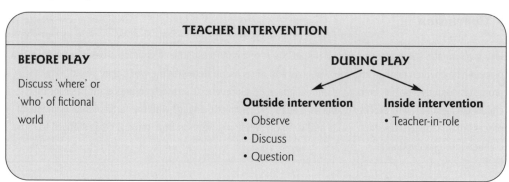

Assessment and Reflection

Children's play is an ongoing process which should take place at an individual's own developmental rate; it is the experience itself which matters. O'Neill effectively summarised this key point in relation to process drama claiming that 'the outcome of the journey is the journey itself, the experience is its own destination' (1995, p. 67). This does not suggest that any learning which takes place is random and without focus. In terms of children's play, a teacher will be seeking to develop potential learning moments which will naturally arise out of the happening of children's play. She will be seeking to develop children cognitively, socially, linguistically and dramatically (see table below).

Asking reflective questions once children have completed their play is a useful way of enabling them to engage in self-refection. This will help children become more consciously aware of the nature of the learning which they have encountered. Questions such as *What did you do today? Did you have any problems? How did you deal with them?* will help in this regard. In addition, these questions can be used to evaluate individual children's progress.

Areas which can be assessed

COGNITIVE	SOCIAL	LANGUAGE	DRAMA
• Theme development • Problem-solving	• Negotiation • Leadership • Sharing	• Turn taking • Sharing (non-verbal) • Listening • Sentence structure • Vocabulary	• Adopt role • Use objects symbolically • Cognitive development while in role

▶ Conclusion

Play is an innate, spontaneous and self-initiated part of a child's early life. It is process-based learning. It is a place where children explore attitudes, feelings and ideas associated with the world they live in. Play promotes cognitive, social, emotional and language development. It provides an important basis for the child's engagement with process drama as it enables the child to engage with the fundamental elements of process drama: belief, role, time, place and symbol. Subtle intervention from the teacher is required to move children into process drama.

Therefore, as children progress through primary school the teacher will take a more active role in the development of content (theme) and form-related knowledge. The remainder of this book will provide those involved in the teaching of drama with practical and theoretical guidelines in relation to using process drama.

Chapter 3
WINTER'S DILEMMA

PART ONE
*A Drama Based on Winter's Dilemma
(First/Second Class)*

PART TWO
Teacher-in-Role

PART ONE: WINTER'S DILEMMA

Background for Teacher

This drama takes place in an Irish forest called Glenmoran. Each year the forest receives four important visitors. Their names are Spring, Summer, Autumn and Winter. These visitors have a very significant impact on the Queen of the Forest (the oldest tree in the forest) and the other plants, animals and people who live there. Each visitor provides an important function in the forest at a particular time in the year. However, this year something very strange has happened, which is causing serious problems in the forest. It seems that the problems have to do with arguments which are taking place between the seasons.

The main focus of the drama is on the children's investigation of the causes and effects of these problems, and on their attempts at trying to improve the situation. Through this work it is hoped that the children will engage cognitively, affectively and artistically with important life themes in the areas of identity, assertiveness and conflict negotiation. The *Winter's Dilemma* story was developed from the initial stimulus of a poem called 'The Thief' by Irene Pawsey.

The second part of the chapter focuses on the convention of *teacher-in-role*, which is a powerful approach to use in the classroom, particularly with young children. It involves the teacher taking on a role in order to both engage children and facilitate their learning from within the drama. The origins of teacher-in-role are explained in terms of both educational and theatre practice. The underlying skills, which are necessary to employing this convention, are explained using particular examples from the *Winter's Dilemma* drama. As teacher-in-role relies just as much on preparation and reflection as it does on the behaviour of the teacher during such moments, each section of this drama is described in terms of:

- Preparation for teacher-in-role
- During teacher-in-role
- Reflection on teacher-in-role

▶ Classroom Sessions

- *Session 1: Building the Context; Confusion in the Forest*
- *Session 2: The Journey to Winter's Den*
- *Session 3: Dealing with the Problem; What Can We Do To Help?*

Three sessions approximately (45 minutes to 1 hour each)

▶ Planning Stimulus

The Thief

by Irene Pawsey

Autumn wind came stealing
Through the woods one day,
And, creeping round the trees he stole
Their beauty all away.

He tore their russet dresses
Cut off their golden hair
He blew away the tattered bits
And left them broken and bare.

As the focus of this drama is on the season of winter, the word winter is used instead of autumn during classroom sessions.

Session 1: Building the Context; Confusion in the Forest

▶ Introduction

- Contract: The teacher tells the children that she has heard that they are very good at solving problems in stories. She then begins to negotiate the drama contract with them. *Would it be possible for you to believe that you are other people in another place for a little while?*

- The children are told that this story takes place in a large forest. The teacher indicates a particular space, which represents the forest during the telling of the story. A large sheet of material could be used for this purpose. While the story is being told, further large pieces of coloured material are placed on the original sheet to represent the seasons as they cover the forest.

▶ The Story: Winter's Dilemma

The Glenmoran Forest had been around for as long as anyone could remember. This very big and old forest was a happy home to the many animals, insects, flowers, and trees that lived there. It was also a happy home to the people of Glenmoran who worked and played there throughout the year. In the centre of the forest lived the oldest and wisest tree. She was known as the Queen of the Forest. She had been there for over one hundred years. Not only was she the oldest and wisest, she was also the tallest and widest tree in the forest. She had a thick trunk, which was so wide it took almost a full day to walk around. Her bark was soft and had green moss living in it. This made it comfortable for the animals and people to lean against when they wanted a rest. Her trunk was so tall that when they went to her for advice, they could hardly see her head. Some said that she was even able to touch the sky with her top branches. The Queen of the Forest felt that she was very lucky to be so tall because she could watch carefully over the whole forest and all who lived there. She was very proud that Glenmoran Forest was known as the happiest forest in the whole of Ireland.

What kind of things do you think the queen could see when she looked around her? What kinds of people, animals, and plants do you think lived there?

Each year the forest had four important visitors. Their names were, Spring, Summer, Autumn and Winter. They took turns at coming to stay in the forest. The Queen of the Forest knew that they each did very important work during their visits, and looked forward to the arrival of each new guest. She had been there for so many years that she knew exactly when to expect each visitor. Like the animals and people, she was always very excited when a new visitor was due to arrive. The visitors travelled a long way from their homes, which were far away from the forest. When it came close to the time for a new visitor to arrive, the queen would stretch her long neck even higher above the trees so that she could catch a glimpse of another one of her old friends coming out of their dens. It was then that she began to send the first rumours of his arrival through the trees.

When it came to the end of the long warm summer, the queen would look far across to the north end of the forest to spot Autumn sleepily crawling out of his den. The first thing Autumn did was to have a big stretch and a big yawn. The old tree thought that Autumn's yawn was almost as long and loud as a bear's. It could be heard for miles around. Over the next few weeks he moved slowly towards the forest and eventually covered it with his large autumnal cloak.

I wonder what happened in the forest when it was covered by Autumn's cloak . . .

Even though Autumn was always a little sleepy, he tried his best to help out over the next few months with all of the collecting and gathering that was needed, so that everybody would be ready for the long winter ahead. After a few months of hard work, the old tree would begin to feel a little chill creeping further into her bark as each day passed. When it came to November the Queen of the Forest was sure that she would not have to wait much longer for her old friend Winter to appear. If she listened carefully enough, she was soon sure to hear the first thud of Winter stumbling out of his den. He plodded noisily and clumsily towards the forest, often bumping into things and knocking things down as he moved.

Winter's cloak always seemed to cover the forest extremely quickly. This was because he usually tripped over it when he arrived. When this happened, the Queen of the Forest giggled to herself because the same thing had happened every year for as long as she could remember!

What do you think happened when the forest was covered by Winter's cloak?

After a while Winter settled quite comfortably into forest life. He made sure that that everyone took a good rest by making it too cold to go out, and by making it impossible for them to do the work that they usually did outdoors. Like everybody else, Winter eventually snuggled down to a long and deep sleep. He was usually quite surprised when it came for his time to leave a few months later. Even the Queen of the Forest, who also tended to be quite sleepy at this time of year, was dazzled by the bright colours which began to beam in the direction of the forest towards the end of January. Soon after that she could hear the familiar sound of Spring singing his little tunes as he skipped along in the direction of the forest. She wondered how Spring could keep so many tunes in his head without repeating a single one.

The queen knew that it would soon be time for everybody to wake up. As he arrived at the edge of the forest Spring became a little quieter, because he had to concentrate on covering every inch of the bare forest with his bright and colourful cloak.

What do you think happened when the forest was covered by Spring's cloak?

After some time went by the queen began to feel more and more heat on her back, which slowly moved down through her bark and warmed up even the skinniest twigs on her younger branches. She could hear the new green leaves giggling together in the warm breeze. When this happened she knew that the last visitor to the forest was on his way. The queen was amused to hear Spring and Summer have a little chatter together as they passed each other on the outskirts of the forest. She sometimes noticed Spring giving a little bow to Summer as they bid farewell. The Queen of the Forest imagined the seasons of the forest would probably be very good friends if they ever got to be in the same place at the same time!

What do you think happened when the forest was covered by Summer's cloak?

▶ Initial signs of a problem

- The children are reminded that the same thing happened in the forest every year. They are then told a shortened version of the story, but this time they are invited to become the inhabitants of the forest as the story is being told. In advance of this activity they may need to engage in a brief discussion about the types of animals, people, plants and trees who might live in the forest. (**Individual mime**)[1]

- When the story has reached its conclusion for the second time, the teacher then narrates: *But one year something very strange happened. The Queen of the Forest looked down at the forest she loved so much, and this is what she saw . . .* (**Narration**)

Children in mime: *A Year in Glenmoran Forest.*

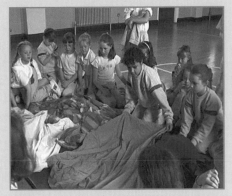

The year that something very strange happened in the forest. ➡

- The teacher jumbles up all of the sheets, which have been used to represent the seasons, so that they are placed in the area simultaneously. The sheet representing Winter covers the smallest amount of space and is situated in the corner. (**Tension**)
- Stimulated by the teacher's questions, the children examine the scene and talk to their partners about what might be happening in the forest, and what the causes might be. These ideas are then shared with the class. (**Discussion in pairs**)

▶ Meeting the Queen of the Forest

Preparation for the teacher-in-role encounter

- The children are told that the queen was very worried about the situation and decided to gather all of the inhabitants of the forest together to discuss the strange event. (**Narration**)

- The teacher explains that she will become the queen for a little while. The children may give advice to the teacher as to where and how she should stand when she becomes queen based on what they have heard about the tree so far.

- The teacher asks the children to suggest a sign to distinguish between when she is in role and when she is the teacher. For example, they might recommend that the teacher should wear a green cloak, stand in a designated space, or hold a branch to show that she has become the Queen of the Forest.

During the teacher-in role encounter

- The teacher-in-role as the queen thanks the children for taking the time to meet her.[2] She explains that she is very worried about the situation in the forest, and is urgently seeking some assistance from people who are good at solving problems e.g. *Have you noticed anything strange happening in the forest lately? What kind of things have you noticed? I wonder why this is happening?* The queen listens carefully to the children's ideas.

- New information can be inserted during the discussion. The teacher-in-role as the queen informs them that she may have found clues which may be of some help. On some of her branches she has found signs posted (adapted version of 'The Thief' by Irene Pawsey p. 41). She has heard from other trees that many of these signs have been posted around the forest. She asks the children if they would like to hear what is written on them. The teacher reads the adapted version of the poem, and also shows them signs which say 'Let's keep Winter out of the forest'. (**Tension**)

- The queen asks the children if they wouldn't mind having a longer think about these clues, and about possible ways of trying to save the forest. She thanks them again for all their hard work and reinforces the need for everyone's help at such a worrying time.

➡

- The teacher comes out of role by removing the sign for the queen of the forest or standing away from the designated space.

Reflection on teacher-in-role encounter

- What new things have we learned about what is going on in the forest?
- What is being said about Winter?
- What other things do you think are being whispered about Winter? (Paired discussion)

▶ How Will We Begin to Deal with the Problem?

- The teacher validates the ideas the children have suggested e.g. *We have come up with a lot of good ideas about what might be going wrong in the forest. How can we be sure that we are right? What do you think we should do next? Would it help to meet anyone else in the story?*

- If the children have not suggested it already, the teacher might suggest a visit to Winter's den in order to get his opinion about what has been happening. When a number of options are put forward by the children in a drama, the teacher will tend to opt for the avenue which provides most potential in terms of both increasing tension and addressing the themes of the drama. The option of visiting Winter also represents the most popular suggestion made by the children in the schools we worked in.

- The teacher asks the children to think of three things they would wear on a journey to Winter's den.

Session 2: The Journey to Winter's Den

▶ Making Links with the Previous Session

- The children help the teacher to represent the visitors to the forest using the pieces of material from the previous session. They add other materials to represent the forest during the year that something very strange happened. (**Defining space**)

And/or

- The children are told that one of the local farmers has been away from the forest for the last year, but since his return he has heard rumours that there have been some problems in Glenmoran Forest that may affect his work. The teacher-in-role as the farmer comes to the villagers to find out what has been going on. (**Teacher-in-role**)

And/or

- Recapping on the context and the problem through questioning and discussion. The children help the teacher to create a chart of words to represent their impressions of Winter's character to date. This can be added to or changed as the drama progresses. (**Role on the wall**)

▶ Getting Ready for the Journey[3]

- The children are reminded that they need to get ready for the very long journey to Winter's den. They discuss how far away from the forest it might be. They discuss what the area might be like around his den.

- In groups the children discuss the kinds of obstacles which they might face on their journey. The teacher uses a large sheet to represent the journey. Each group decides on one difficult obstacle to be overcome and creates a drawing which will represent this obstacle. They then make a decision with regard to where it will be placed on the class model of their journey. (**Paper placement,** see photo p. 47)

- After examining the model carefully the teacher asks each child to go away and find the clothes and shoes that they think would be most appropriate to wear on the journey (**mime**). Each child should also pack his bag for the journey. They should be reminded that the bag cannot be too heavy as there may be a lot of walking and climbing to be done. Therefore, apart from food and clothes, they can only bring three special things which they think will be useful. (**Individual mime**)

- With the help of the teacher the children could devise a rhyme or slogan which would help them at difficult stages of the journey. (**Rhymes/slogans**)

- The children now embark on their journey. They physically respond to the various stages of the journey as they are announced. These will be based on the ideas which emerged during the previous exercise. The rhyme or slogan can also be used at difficult stages in the journey. When the teacher finally points at what she thinks is Winter's den in the distance, the children describe what they see. Appropriate background music can be used to enhance the experience if desired. (**Mime supported by narration**)

▶ Meeting Winter

Preparation for teacher-in-role

- The children have finally reached Winter's den after a long and difficult journey and they know they will soon meet him. (**Narration**)

- The children create Winter's den.

  — The children discuss what they imagine Winter's den might be like inside e.g. *What kind of things would Winter keep in his den? What would his bed be like? Would he decorate the walls? How would he decorate them?* (**Discussion**)

  — The children advise the teacher as to how some of the furniture of the classroom may be used to begin to create Winter's den. The teacher follows these directions with the help of individual children. (**Defining space**)

  ➤

— Each child is given two pieces of paper and crayons, and is asked to draw examples of the personal items which would be in Winter's den. Each child then places his item in a particular part of Winter's den. (**Paper placement**)

— In the event that children create items which give a negative impression only of Winter, the teacher can insert a number of items which would add more complexity to Winter's character e.g. picture of summer, birthday card for spring. (**Tension**)

• The children make recommendations as to how they think Winter would dress, move or sit in his den. They are asked to choose the cloak (from the original pieces of material) which they think Winter would wear. (**Costume**)

• The teacher explains to the children that she would like them to watch Winter alone in his den for a few minutes. In role as Winter she then demonstrates a short mime sequence of Winter in his den. Winter displays behaviour that suggests that he is very confused and worried. He is also distracted by a large piece of paper which is lying on the ground.[4] He eventually looks at it, is upset by it and crumples it up. (**Mime**)

• The teacher comes out of role and asks the children for their response to the previous sequence e.g. *Did we learn anything new about Winter? What kind of mood was he in? What gave you the idea that this was the case? What could he be worried about? What would you like to ask Winter when you meet him?*

During teacher-in-role encounter

• The children ask Winter questions based on their curiosities.[5]

Paper placement: creating Winter's den

• The teacher-in-role as Winter, who is perhaps initially unsure about whether to trust the children, eventually informs them of the things the other seasons have been doing to him and saying about him behind his back. Everybody seems to be ignoring him and when it is his turn to be in the forest, they try to push him out, *especially* Summer. He tells them that he cannot understand why they are doing this to him.

• Winter asks the children to help him to think of the reasons he does the things he does. The teacher can help them here if they are having difficulty e.g. *I thought it was my job to blow things down and bring cold weather so that everyone can have a rest, and have Christmas.*

➡

- If the children request it, Winter shows them the latest signs which he found stuck to the trees around the forest. They include the poem 'The Thief' and the signs saying, 'Let's keep Winter out of the forest'. Unlike the original signs, which were shown to them by the queen, these particular signs have been signed by Summer.

- Winter asks the children for their advice about what he should do. He emphasises that he will need help with implementing their suggestions, as he is now feeling very afraid and nervous about talking to people, and about leaving his den.

After teacher-in-role encounter

- The teacher helps the children to reflect on the teacher-in-role encounter using the role on the wall which they have developed previously. She adds to or changes the contents of this list as instructed by the children. (**Role on the wall**)

- Between this and the next session, the teacher suggests that the children write a letter to the Queen of the Forest to inform her about what they have found out from their meeting with Winter, and to make suggestions for what should be done next.[6] (**Letter writing**)

Session 3: Dealing with the Problem

▶ *Making Links with the Previous Session*

- The teacher reads the children a letter which has been sent to them by the Queen of the Forest. In this letter, the queen thanks them for their hard work and attempts to respond to the various ideas and suggestions which they sent in their letter. She tells them that things have become very serious in the forest since she spoke to them last. It is now nearly the end of December and Winter hasn't arrived yet. All of the other seasons have remained in the forest together and everyone is very confused about what they are supposed to be doing. The weather is changing all the time. The animals and people are exhausted. She suggests that Winter should try to speak to Summer as soon as possible to sort out the problem before the forest is destroyed. She informs them that a letter has also been sent to both Winter and Summer suggesting a meeting near Glenmoran Lake in a week's time.

- To explore the importance of Winter as a season, the children create still images in pairs or threes based on a year in the forest without Winter. (**Still image**)[7]

◗ Winter Confronts Summer

(Adaptation of Forum Theatre)[8]

Preparation for teacher-in-role encounter

- The teacher narrates that after a lot of persuasion from the queen, Winter has finally agreed to meet Summer. She discusses with them his preparation for the journey, and how he might have been feeling as he left his den on the morning of the meeting. The children help to set up the space where the meeting between the two characters will take place. The teacher places the representative cloaks for Winter and Summer on two facing chairs. The teacher explains that the children will be Winter and that she will be Summer.[9] (**Place**)

- To help the children to get into the role of Winter, they review the role on the wall chart which was created previously (**Role on the wall**). The teacher then encourages them all to put on their 'Winter cloaks'. (**Mime**)

- Arrangement: The children sit in a semi-circle behind the chair representing Winter. The teacher sits on the chair representing Summer.

- The children are asked about what they, as Winter, would like to say to Summer. They are asked about what difficulties they expect during this meeting and how they might overcome them. (**Collective role**)

During teacher-in-role encounter

- The teacher begins by playing a very arrogant Summer who clearly looks down on Winter and is very confident about his own behaviour in the forest in recent times. (**Building tension**)

Examples of teacher talk:

- *I was very surprised to hear that you wanted to speak to me. I am very busy so I would appreciate if you would get on with what you have to say as quickly as possible.*

- *I don't understand what you are so upset about? We had no choice but to exclude you. Do you realise all the work the rest of the seasons have to do in the forest after all the damage and laziness you leave behind? What do you have to offer in comparison with my heat, light and immense colour?* (**Tension**)

Pauses for reflection

The teacher can pause the proceedings at various stages if necessary, to help the children to reflect on the encounter so far, e.g. *How do you feel the meeting is going with Summer so far? Are you happy that you have said everything you want to say to Summer? Would you change anything if you had the chance to go back to a certain part of the meeting again?*

➡

Resuming the meeting

- The teacher goes back to the part of the meeting as requested by the children. The teacher, as Summer, begins this section by repeating the statements which the children would like to confront.

- The meeting is re-run until the children are happy that they have received an acceptable improvement in the conflict between Winter and Summer.

- If the children, as Winter, have done a good job at articulating their feelings about Summer's behaviour and explaining the necessity of having a winter every year (the teacher shouldn't make this too easy for them!), Summer may eventually acknowledge that they may have a point. If this is the case, Summer asks the children what they would like him to say or do now. In the school we worked in, the teacher-in-role as Summer eventually acknowledged that she did not know that Winter felt like this. However, the children insisted that he should offer Winter an apology.

After teacher-in-role encounter

- Possible questions for reflection. *How do you feel the meeting went with Summer? Are you happy with the outcome? Was there anything you were surprised about? What do you think will happen next? How do you think Winter felt after the meeting? What did you think of Summer's behaviour during the meeting?*

Adaptation of Forum Theatre: 'Winter meets Summer'

▶ *Follow-up Activities*

- The children create a new cloak for Winter onto which pictorial or symbolic reminders of what makes him special are attached.

- Summer/Winter write their thoughts in their diaries on the evening of their meeting.

- The children return to the forest a year later to hear from the inhabitants how things have been going since the unusual incidents of the previous year. More experienced groups might work in pairs for this activity, one as a newspaper reporter and one as an inhabitant of the forest. (**Paired improvisation**)[10]

Examples of ways in which this drama has been integrated with other subject areas:

Integration and *Winter's Dilemma*

SECTION OF *WINTER'S DILEMMA* DRAMA	SUBJECT/STRAND	SKILLS
• Story: *Winter's Dilemma*	English Strand: Receptiveness to language	• Listening and responding to stories.
• Roll on the wall of Winter's character	English Strand: Emotional and imaginative development through language	• Predicting and hypothesising with regard to unfinished areas of the story. • Oral language development. • Character analysis.
• Mime of activities in the forest throughout the year	Geography Strand: The natural environment; Environmental awareness and care	• Naming the seasons, identifying the months that are in each season, identifying the changes in nature which are associated with each season.
	Physical Education Strand: Dance	• Using the body to express ideas and feelings. • Developing a vocabulary for physical activity.
• Constructing the inside of Winter's den using symbolic materials	Geography Strand: Natural environments	• Spatial awareness and map making.
	Art Strand: Construction	• Construction
• Collective role: Winter meets Summer. Analysing Winter's feelings after the TIR mime sequence	SPHE Strand: Myself and others	• Exploring and understanding the nature of conflict, trying out various strategies in context.
• Further possibilities for integration	Music Strand: Composing	• Creating a sound collage using real or imaginary instruments based on the year that something very strange happened in the forest.

PART TWO: TEACHER-IN-ROLE

> *I am constantly amazed by the miracle of how thinking about a dramatic idea can in an instant become that of carrying it into action. There is a world of difference between someone in class saying, 'Well, they would all take their belongings with them' and saying 'Let's pack up and leave'.*
>
> (Heathcote, 1984, p. 160)

What Is Teacher-in-role?

At various stages in the *Winter's Dilemma* drama, the teacher interacts with the children as a particular character from the story. When she interacts with them as the queen, as Winter or as Summer, she is employing the convention of teacher-in-role. This very powerful approach allows her to stimulate and intrigue children in a unique fashion, while also challenging them to explore human themes and issues from within the drama. The experience of interacting in the 'now time' (a term used by Dorothy Heathcote) has the effect of engaging children on an emotional and intellectual level simultaneously. They tend to enjoy the sense of learning, without necessarily being conscious that they are learning, which ensues from such an approach.

Children also tend to enjoy interacting with their teacher on a very different level through teacher-in-role. In general, it is not often that children have the opportunity to challenge or negotiate with a teacher who does not know what to do, or whose actions they may not completely approve of! For example, in the *Winter's Dilemma* they meet their teacher as a character who seems helpless in the face of another's bullying tactics, but also as the instigator of these actions who seems oblivious of their harsh effects. The use of teacher-in-role can be a very effective way of handing over responsibility to children for the direction of the drama.

▶ Engaging the Children when in Role

As a process drama is negotiated and constructed collaboratively between the teacher and the children, it is generally not necessary for the teacher to take on the full characterisation we tend to associate with traditional acting styles, such as precise costuming, specific accents, make-up and so on. Participants in a process drama do not tend to rely on such detail for their belief because they have already agreed to believe in the process, and have often assisted in the creation of the teacher's role themselves. However, as is the case with all types of acting, a certain level of belief, integrity and manipulation of verbal and non-verbal signals is needed on the part of the teacher in order to adequately engage children during the encounter itself. In her planning, it can be helpful for the teacher to consider carefully the variety of social roles that she and others occupy in daily life, in terms of the signals, language, and contexts within which such roles operate. For example, in her own life she may embody the various roles of teacher, mother, friend, wife, musician and so on. Careful reflection on these and other roles will bring the awareness that each role affects communication with others in a particular way. This knowledge, alongside the teacher's manipulation of fundamental theatre elements such as belief and tension, will provide the basis for her engagement with teacher-in-role.

As is the case with teaching generally, each teacher will develop her own style in this area depending on her personality and on her increasing experience of the art form. In the following sections we will discuss important considerations to be taken into account when preparing for, engaging in and reflecting on a teacher-in-role encounter with children.

Preparing for a Teacher-in-role Encounter

❱ *Preparing the children*

Teachers' fears with regard to teacher-in-role are often alleviated when they begin to recognise the effects of developing children's belief in the role *in advance* of the encounter. Because such encounters are essentially improvisational, this preparation tends to take place in an indirect manner. For example, the children's initial understanding of the character of Winter is developed when they mime the variety of activities that take place in the forest during the course of one year. Also, in the direct lead up to their meeting with Winter, the children become even more invested in his character as they create the particular features of his den, and give advice to the teacher about how she should dress and move as Winter when she is in role.

❱ *Teacher preparation*

In Chapter 2, Planning and Facilitation, we discussed the notion that the teacher will have a dual focus within any drama experience, in that she continually needs to be aware of both the *levels of engagement* of the children, and opportunities for *thematic exploration* throughout. This principle will apply to all moments, but it is particularly relevant for our consideration of teacher-in-role. Later we will concentrate on the ways in which the teacher can engage and intrigue the children during the encounter while also maintaining some level of focus. However, careful consideration of the following issues in *advance* of the encounter will also help to provide the teacher with the confidence and support she needs on both levels. While a teacher-in-role encounter is not scripted in advance, this does not deny us any preparation whatsoever!

❱ *Attitude*

The teacher usually identifies an attitude which she would like to communicate during the meeting. Her choice of attitude is usually directly related to the main themes of the drama, which in this case focused on assertiveness and identity. For example, during the children's first meeting with Winter, the teacher takes a helpless attitude towards the group. She does this in the hope that they will both empathise with Winter, and begin to explore ways of improving his situation. When the teacher is later in role as Summer she takes a challenging attitude towards the children as Winter, so that they will have to defend themselves clearly against Summer's bullying tactics.

▶ *Function*

As is the case with many characters in a theatrical encounter, the teacher-in-role usually meets the group with some purpose. This may take the form of new information to be imparted, a tension to be inserted, a cry for help, or a task to be issued. While the teacher-in-role may have a general purpose in meeting with the children, it is not for her to decide how they should respond. Usually the most productive teacher-in-role encounters are those which are provocative and complex enough to yield a variety of responses from the children.

▶ *Tension*

Later we will discuss the ways in which tension can be inserted during the encounter itself. However, it must be remembered that the tensions which are present in the drama *before* the encounter, can also provide important motivation for children's engagement with a particular role. As a result of the underlying tensions of a drama, we often find that children request to meet certain characters before it is suggested by the teacher. For example, in the schools we worked in, the anticipation and desire to meet Summer was very strong in the children towards the end of the drama. This was because they had ample evidence of the negative effects of Summer's behaviour on the inhabitants of the forest, and on the character of Winter.

Preparation for teacher-in-role Example I

ROLE	ATTITUDE	FUNCTION	TENSION
The Queen of the Forest meets the children for the first time	Worried, concerned, in need of help and advice	• To organise a plan of action • To give the children more information about the problem • To enlist their help • To listen to their ideas about what is going on in the forest	*Before encounter* The children have been told that this year something very strange has happened in the forest. The material which has been used to represent the seasonal activity in the forest is suddenly presented in a chaotic form.

▶ *Status*

Status in a teacher-in-role encounter refers to the power relationship between the teacher's character and the group. The teacher's role is usually categorised in terms of high, middle and low status roles. These distinctions tend to be based on the structures upon which society traditionally operates and/or the particular circumstances of a character at a particular time in the drama. For example, in the *Tom Crean* drama (Chapter 5), the teacher is in a high status role when she as captain meets with her crew to organise an important expedition. Depending on her purpose, she may alternatively opt to take a low status role and become a new crew member who needs to find out about the tasks and responsibilities involved in preparing for such an important Arctic expedition. The teacher's choice of status tends to relate to the level of responsibility that she wishes to hand over to the children at a particular point in the drama.

▶ High Status Roles

Typical functions: to organise, to co-ordinate, to give orders, to give information
The teacher usually chooses such roles when she would like to co-ordinate and organise within the drama. High status roles tend to include kings, queens, government leaders, heads of organisations, captains of boats, co-ordinators of expeditions and so on. These roles have the additional advantage of allowing teachers to maintain focus and discipline from within the role. As can often be the case with high status roles, the queen in the *Winter's Dilemma* can also become a supporting character with whom the children can discuss new information and new courses of action.[11]

▶ Middle Status Roles

Typical functions: to discuss, to negotiate, to play devil's advocate, to give information
These characters usually have the same amount of power as the group in terms of implementing change and making decisions. Examples of middle status roles are fellow workers, those who are second-in-command, or those who take the role of reporters or researchers within a given situation. When interacting with a middle status role, children are more likely to challenge the status quo, and to freely voice opinions about the current situation e.g. teacher-in-role as Summer interacting with the children-in-role as Winter.

▶ Low Status Roles

Typical functions: to seek help, to seek advice, to give information
The teacher takes on a low status role when she would like the children to take a lot of responsibility within the drama. In such a role the teacher may come to the children looking for their help, advice or expertise. Examples of low status roles might include visitors to a community, characters who have little expertise in a particular area, or characters who have been ostracised. For example, in this drama the teacher-in-role takes on a low status role when she as Winter requires assistance because of the disturbing things that have happened in the forest. Children tend to enjoy interacting with such roles due to the level of expertise which is assumed of them during the encounter.

Preparation for teacher-in-role Example 2

ROLE	STATUS	ATTITUDE	PURPOSE	TENSION
TIR as Winter (first meeting)	Low	Hopeless, unhappy, needing help	• To inform the children of how he is being treated • To ask for their help in making things better	**Before encounter** • The Queen of the Forest needs their help and has asked them to find out what is wrong with Winter • During the mime sequence Winter ripped up a piece of paper in a rage

During teacher-in-role

While the last section focused on the type of *preparation* which can positively affect a teacher-in-role encounter, this section refers to the skills and strategies which can be employed during the encounter itself in order to both enhance participation and provide thematic focus for the work.

▶ *Belief*

The teacher's belief in the role and in the situation is directly related to that of the children. A teacher's initial steps into role are likely to be very unusual for the children, particularly for those who are unfamiliar with this convention. It is important to continue to maintain a serious commitment to the role particularly at this early stage. The teacher's belief in the role is communicated to the children through confident and clear verbal and non-verbal signals. This usually has the effect of reassuring children that the teacher will stay in role if they risk a contribution.

▶ *Objects and props*

The use of a simple prop such as a scarf or a hat can be a useful aid in helping both the teacher and pupils to make the transition into the fiction. In *Winter's Dilemma* the teacher chooses a coloured sheet to indicate when she is becoming one of the seasons. Whatever the gesture she uses to indicate the move into role, it is most important that she explains clearly the rules of the convention which is about to be employed. Otherwise children can become confused about the distinction between fiction and reality. At all stages of the *Winter's Dilemma*, the teacher pre-empts her move into role just before it happens e.g. *When I put the navy sheet around me, I will become Winter, when I take it off again I will be the teacher*.

▶ *Non-verbal signals*

The teacher's careful reflection on the particular character in question, and on the various social roles she is familiar with, will generally help her to find the necessary signals from her own communication repertoire to demonstrate belief and authenticity when in role. However, as she becomes more experienced she will become more consciously aware of the impact of her non-verbal signals in terms of communicating messages and provoking responses from the children. Consider the impact of an unexpected silence as the teacher scans the group for accomplices, the raising of her eyebrows to show suspicion or surprise, or the look of confusion and dismay as she reads a long awaited letter. Signals of this kind can often communicate far more than direct statements during a meeting with a role.

▶ Validating responses

In the early stages of a teacher-in-role encounter the children will be watching the teacher carefully for signs that she is going to continue to take the role and the situation seriously if a contribution is made from the group. Therefore she must be particularly careful to validate meaningfully their early contributions. Of course this will be done as the character rather than as the teacher. There are a number of ways in which the teacher can acknowledge the child's belief and level of thinking, which may be more natural to the role than more direct affirmations such as 'very good' or 'well done'. In general, the teacher should try to respond to children with a remark which will both validate the contribution given and simultaneously encourage or provoke further contributions from the group. In this way the teacher ensures that the conversation does not die before the key issues have been raised and explored.

Example: teacher-in-role as the queen of the forest
That's a very interesting way of looking at it. I hadn't thought about it like that before, so do you think we should just ignore what the other seasons are doing? What do other people think about that?

▶ Inserting Tension

In the section on preparation for teacher-in-role, the importance of developing an overall tension within a drama was discussed. However some encounters may require the insertion of further tensions during the encounter itself. Let us take the example of the children's meeting with the Queen of the Forest. In contrast with their later meeting with Summer, they are unlikely to have the same urgent desire to meet the queen, particularly at this early stage of the drama. This is partly because they do not know anything about her and partly because there does not seem to be a *need* to meet her. The following are examples of the various ways in which the teacher can insert tension into the encounter in order to both initiate and increase participation. You will notice that some requests for participation are more direct than others. Depending on the situation, an indirect request implied within a statement can sometimes be even more effective than a direct question in terms of provoking responses.

- Direct: The teacher shows them the symbolic representation of the confusion in the forest. She demonstrates her concern for the wellbeing of the inhabitants and asks them directly for their help, and for their suggestions.

- Indirect: Tension is introduced through the phrasing of the teacher's statements e.g. *I wonder what could have caused such chaos in the forest. I wonder why the seasons are so angry with Winter. I really don't know who I could call on to be brave enough to deal with a problem as complicated as this one.*

Tension can also be increased during the encounter by providing a contrast between the type of character the children *expect* to meet, and the character they actually meet. For example, perhaps Summer has some new information to share with the children which could throw a new light on the situation. At the end of the drama the teacher could decide to play Summer in a very reasonable manner by putting forward the notion that she has actually been misunderstood.

▶ *Behaviour Management*

Both the collaborative building of context and clarity around the rules of drama during the contract stage will generally tend to prevent any serious behavioural problems during a teacher-in-role encounter. However, the following advice may be helpful if difficulties arise.

Firstly what the teacher may perceive as indiscipline during the early stages of a meeting, may often represent an understandable nervousness or excitement among the children, or a desire to test her commitment to the role. In our experience even contributions which may seem a little unusual, or to contain an element of subversion, in the early stages should appear to be taken seriously if at all possible. Facilitated skilfully, they may even indirectly help to move the drama onto another stage.

> **Example**
>
> Teacher-in-role as queen: *So how do you think Winter should deal with Summer?*
> Paul (pupil): *I think Winter should kick Summer in the head.*
>
> Teacher-in-role as queen to Paul: *So you think that Winter should confront Summer then? That sounds like an interesting idea. Do you think Winter would be up to that? You did say he seemed a little nervous before. Still, a meeting between them might be worth a try. Thank you Paul.*
>
> Teacher-in-role as queen to group: *If we encourage Winter to meet Summer as has been suggested, it seems like we will have to give him a lot of help. What do you think the other seasons would think of Winter if he kicked Summer in the head? How should we advise him to approach the meeting?'*

This approach usually has the effect of channelling the apparent attempt at subversion. The teacher here is showing a positive expectation in relation to the child's contribution which can allow him another chance to contribute constructively later in the discussion.

However, there may be some occasions when it is necessary for the teacher to come out of role for a short period to reassess the children's understanding of and commitment to the situation e.g. *Do you think that this is the way the inhabitants of the forest would speak to a queen? How do you think a queen would usually be addressed?* Sometimes teachers raise concerns about the calling out of answers during an encounter, which makes it difficult for others to hear and to speak. Often such issues can also be addressed effectively from within the role e.g. *As you know it is the custom at meetings with the Queen of the Forest that two people cannot speak at the same time.*

If the children's overall belief in the drama has been established prior to the meeting with the role, the above strategies should prove effective in helping to focus the children's attention constructively on the situation.

After Teacher-in-role

When do I come out of role?
Drama by its nature has the tendency to complicate and to challenge easy answers to life issues. The general aim of a teacher-in-role encounter is that children begin to become aware of the complexity of a given situation as they explore it from various angles. The teacher generally comes out of role when she feels this aim has been achieved. She should not feel that the children are required to solve or agree on all issues during the encounter itself.

How do I come out of role?
The teacher usually signals that she has come out of role by removing the symbol which the children have learned to associate with her character e.g. taking off the cloak.

When working with younger children or children who are inexperienced in the area of drama, it can also be necessary for the teacher to state verbally that she has come out of role and that she is now their teacher again. Moving to a different area of the room can also help in this regard.

Reflection
Reflection on a teacher-in-role encounter is essential in terms of ascertaining new information and insights about the character or situation. These insights are often crucial to their overall understanding of the drama. After the children's first meeting with Winter, the teacher might probe the children's perceptions of Winter with questions such as *How do you feel about Winter now? Did you expect him to be this way? What new things did you learn about Winter?* You will notice from these questions that the teacher refers to the character in the third person when she is out of role. This convention allows the children more liberty to discuss the character openly, and reinforces the distinction between fiction and reality. The children can also reflect on a teacher-in-role experience through another teacher-in-role encounter or through another moment in the drama. For example, the children we worked with found it helpful to report back to the queen about their meeting with Winter, and to discuss his characteristics through the convention of role on the wall.

▶ Summary

- Teacher-in-role is a powerful convention, which allows the children to engage with both character and theme in an exiting and interactive manner.

- Before teacher-in-role: While teacher-in-role is improvisational in nature, the advance identification of a character's attitude, function and status are helpful guides to the teacher during the encounter.

- During teacher-in-role: The teacher's ability to believe in and engage the children with the character is directly related to their belief and participation during the encounter. In this regard the teacher relies on the power of her verbal and non-verbal skills, as she manipulates significant theatre elements such as belief, tension and the use of props.

- After the teacher-in-role encounter, it is important for children to reflect on new insights or information gained about the character and situation. This can be done effectively through direct discussion or through the use of another drama convention.

Footnotes

1 Please refer to the section on working physically in drama in Chapter 5 for additional support.

2 The children may either be themselves during this encounter, or assume the roles which they created during the mime section earlier e.g. animals or trees. If they do not go into the fictional role of inhabitants, they can nonetheless be 'themselves in role as experts' who are good at solving problems (Bowell and Heap, 2001, p. 85). This approach is drawn from Dorothy Heathcote's 'Mantle of the Expert' approach. When children are given such generic expert roles in a drama Toye and Prenderville (2000) refer to them as 'superhelpers'.

3 Eileen Pennington's invaluable advice and guidance in relation to doing physical work with young children. (ADEI Workshop, Trinity College, Dublin, 2002)

4 The children will later find out that this sheet contains negative statements which others have posted around the forest about Winter.

5 Examples of questions used in the schools we worked in included: *Why are you so mean? Why do you blow everything down? Do you have a problem?*

6 This could be created as a class letter using the language experience approach (LEA).

7 See Chapter 6 for more guidance in relation to facilitating still images in the classroom.

8 In the 1970s Augusto Boal developed a theatre form in Brazil known as forum theatre. This approach allowed a group to participate and effect change in a live performance. The content of the performance is usually based on a situation of oppression, which is representative of the experience of the participants. However it has been adapted in a variety of ways within process drama situations, and in such contexts it is usually based on a fictional situation.

9 When working with younger children, or groups who need more support, the teacher could go into role as a fearful or unsure Winter before the meeting, and ask them for some last minute advice.

10 Please see the second part of Chapter 5 for additional support in the area of paired improvisation.

11 It is important to note that the functions listed in each section are those which are typical of roles of a certain status. However, they are not exclusive to these roles and much will depend on the teacher's objectives for a given situation. For example, the queen while having a high status in the forest was in reality using many of the functions of a middle status role.

Chapter 4
THE CHILDREN OF LIR

PART ONE

*A Drama Based on The Children of Lir
(Third/Fourth/Fifth Class)*

PART TWO

Working Physically in Drama

PART ONE: A DRAMA BASED ON THE CHILDREN OF LIR

Background for Teacher

This drama is based on a very old and popular Irish legend called *The Children of Lir*, which is part of the mythological cycle of Irish stories. This is a tale in which four children find themselves transformed into swans by their new stepmother Aoife, who is jealous of their relationship with their father Lir. This drama, which explores the themes of change, jealousy and family, has a double purpose. Firstly it is designed to allow the children to explore the moments before, during and after this event, so that they can attempt to empathise with and respond to the various characters and incidents of the story. As is the case with all process drama, they can also change and transform the story. The second aim of the drama, which is addressed simultaneously, is to allow the children to develop their individual capacity to express themselves and to communicate through physical image-making and creative movement.

The drama section of this chapter is structured in a slightly different way to the other dramas in this book, in that it begins by presenting two context-building sessions which form a starting point for the drama only. These are followed by a variety of options for progression depending on the desired emphasis of further sessions, and on the drama experience of the children. Some of the options are presented in more detail than others. These include options which particularly illustrate how children might be helped to explore movement, symbol and text as vehicles for both expression and representation in drama. The options which are discussed in less detail are those which are explored more thoroughly elsewhere in this book.

The second part of the chapter includes a rationale for the physical emphasis in all drama, which is based on theatrical and educational principles. It also highlights the skills which are inherent in facilitating such work in the classroom. This is done through giving specific guidance around the preparation for, improvisation in and sharing of image work, movement and dance. Particular examples from *The Children of Lir* drama will be used for illustration.

▶ *Classroom Sessions*

- *Session 1: Introducing the Story; Meeting Machaomog*
- *Session 2: Building the Context; Aoife's Memories*
- *Options: Possibilities for Progression*
- *Options: Opportunities for Poetic Action*

Planning Source for the Teacher

❭ The Children of Lir: Irish Folktale from the Mythological Cycle

A summary of *The Children of Lir* is provided below.[1] The teacher can use this as a basis for the improvised storytelling which takes place in Session 1.

Summary of story

This story is about a family who lived in the north-western part of Ireland a long, long time ago. After the death of his wife, Lir remarried a woman called Aoife, who became a stepmother to his four children, Fionnuala, Conn, Aod and Fiachra. Aoife soon became jealous of Lir's relationship with his children. One day she decided to bring the children for a swim in Lake Derravaragh. When the children were immersed in the water she cast a wicked spell on them which was to last for nine hundred years. She changed the children into swans and cast them out onto the wild waters of Ireland. She told them that they would spend three hundred years at each of the following places: Lake Derravaragh, The Sea of Moyle and Inish Glora. They would not regain their human form until a king from the North married a queen from the South, and until they heard a loud bell heralding a new faith over the country of Ireland. When Fionnuala begged Aoife for mercy, Aoife told them that they would keep their hearts and voices and that their music would console all who heard them. Shocked by her deed, Aoife ran to her chariot and galloped away.

Later that day Lir was passing Lake Derravaragh and he heard his children's voices calling to him. As he listened to them, he became devastated by what had happened. The children spent nine hundred difficult years fighting the winds and the storms on the waters of Ireland, but as Aoife had predicted they consoled each other and all who heard them with their sweet music. The story of the children of Lir became known throughout Ireland and was passed down from generation to generation. After nine hundred years, a new age had dawned in Ireland. Machaomog, a hermit of the Christian faith had a particular interest in the story and built a little church on Inish Glora where he waited and prayed for the children. In that particular year, a king from the North married a queen from the South. One day after Machaomog said his prayers, he rang out a large bronze bell, and he began to hear the children's singing coming towards him. He watched with sadness as the swans turned into very old men and women and he took care of their feeble bodies until their death the following morning.

Session 1: Introducing the Story; Meeting Machaomog

❭ Introduction

- Creating the atmosphere: The children enter a slightly darkened room (blinds closed, lights off) and are asked to sit in a circle on the floor. One or more images containing characters, patterns or artefacts from Irish legends have been placed on the wall. A simple lighted candle is placed at the side of the room. (**Place**)[2]

➡

- The teacher helps the children to 'read' one of the images on the wall. This could be a less well-known image from *The Children of Lir* story or another Celtic story. With the help of the teacher's questions, the children are asked to 'wonder' about the place, time, character motivations and previous events related to this picture. It is emphasised that there are no right answers within this type of activity. (**Preparation for image work**)

- The teacher discusses the issue of belief with the children. *Would it be possible for you to believe that you are other people in another place for a little while?* (**Contract**)

- The children are told that one of the main characters in this drama is a character called Machaomog, a hermit who lived on a little island called Inish Glora around the time of St Patrick. The teacher may wish to have a discussion with the children with regard to their knowledge of this period, and the location and imagined context of Inish Glora. Photographs, paintings, maps and artefacts can be examined here to extend their knowledge of the period. She tells them that Machaomog has a very mysterious story to tell them.

▶ Machaomog's Story

In this section, the teacher will be telling the story of *The Children of Lir* to the pupils, while in role as Machaomog. The bones of this story are provided on p. 63.

Preparation for teacher-in-role encounter
- The teacher uses the information from the discussion above to help move the children's imaginations into the context of Inish Glora. The teacher asks them to close their eyes and to imagine sitting just outside Machaomog's hut, e.g. *What can you hear around you? What are you sitting on? What does it feel like?* (**Guided imagery**)

- The teacher explains to the children that when she puts on her large cloak, she will become Machaomog, and when she takes it off again she will be herself.

- The teacher moves away from the circle, puts on the large cloak and returns to the circle with the lighted candle which she places at the centre of the circle.

During teacher-in-role encounter
- Machaomog (teacher-in-role) sits on the ground with the children and tells them why he is here. He would like to tell them about an unusual thing that happened to him a few weeks ago, an event that was so special and beautiful that he can't stop thinking about it. *Would you mind if I shared this story with you as I have not had anyone else to talk to about it on this lonely island? I am afraid that if I don't tell it to somebody, it will be forgotten forever.*

- Machaomog tells them that this story begins nine hundred years ago. The teacher-in-role as Machaomog tells the story of *The Children of Lir* from his perspective. (**Storytelling**)

Teacher-in-role: Machaomog's story

After teacher-in-role encounter
Responding to the story through image and movement

In this drama, the children's opportunities for exploration through movement and dance represent the interplay between structure and freedom which is characteristic of much drama and dance activity. You will notice that the earlier suggestions in emphasis involve more support for the children in their explorations. The transformation from children to swans through dance, which will be discussed later in the chapter, leans in emphasis towards a more improvised approach. The basis for such progression will be discussed in the second part of this chapter.

- The children are reminded that Machaomog told the story through words. *What other way could he have told the story?* It is explained that we can also tell stories using our bodies. The teacher demonstrates a still image and afterwards asks the children to talk about what could be read from it. The children may notice that when reading images in this way, many meanings can be interpreted from one image and many meanings can be created. (**Preparation for image work**)

- *Do you think that it would now be possible for you to help Machaomog to tell his story through pictures or images with your body?* The children are first asked to walk around the room in different directions. In advance of this walk they are told that when the teacher claps, she will give them five seconds to create an image of one moment from the story that interested them. (**Image – individual**)

- The children carry out this task twice. They are then asked to find a partner. One decides he is number one, and the other number two. Each child's task is to teach his second image to his partner

➡

through *demonstration* with as much accuracy as possible.[3] Each pair should then have two images which they can demonstrate. The children then name their images – image one and image two. After giving them a period of exploration, the teacher explains that when she claps the first time, they should create image one, and when she claps again, they should create image two. (**Creating a sequence of images in pairs.**)

- The children are now asked to gradually move from image one to image two over a period of ten seconds. They should begin in image one. They are told that the teacher will count down from ten to one and that by the time she gets to one they should have moved into image two. When they have taken ten seconds to move from image one to image two, they can immediately take another ten seconds to move back into image one again. (**Preparation for movement**)

- The teacher explains that the next time they do this movement she will play a piece of music which will help them in their movement, and she will not speak. After this section, the teacher asks the children to discuss their responses to this activity with their partner. (**Preparation for dance**)

- The teacher asks one half of the class to sit on the floor, while the other half share their movement pieces. The teacher encourages the observers to respond to the emotional, narrative and aesthetic aspects of what they have seen. *How did you feel when you were watching that piece of movement? What words or images came to mind? What did you notice about the way other people were moving?* The teacher draws their attention to changes in height, speed and flow.[4] The same activity is repeated with the other half of the class. (**Sharing**)

Responding to the story through movement

Chapter 4 THE CHILDREN OF LIR

Session 2: Building the Context; Aoife's Memories

▶ *Exploring the Character of Aoife*

Introduction

- The children's attention is drawn to the day that Aoife cast a spell on the children. They are asked particularly to think about the morning time, when she woke up. One of the first things she did was to take a look around at her room. *What kind of room do you think Aoife had? What are the walls like? What is the furniture like? What is it made of? What kinds of decorations, pictures and objects are in the room?* After a few moments, the children are asked to open their eyes and to discuss their imaginings with their partner. (**Guided imagery**)

- Each child is asked to find a spot in the room to lie down in and to close his eyes. He is asked to consider the following questions without answering them out loud. *What kind of mood do you think Aoife was in that day? What, do you think, was she wearing that day? What colour, do you think, did she decide to wear?* In their own time the children are asked to become Aoife as she gets up that morning and makes her preparations for the day ahead. The teacher then allows the children some time to immerse themselves in this activity. (**Individual mime**)

- When she feels that they have explored the above activity adequately the teacher asks them to freeze, and to hold their position for the next few minutes. While they are frozen she begins the following voice-over. *As Aoife prepared herself carefully for the day ahead, she began to think about her memories of the previous few weeks and of all the incidents that had happened in the Lir household that made her more and more certain that she must do something to change things in the house forever.* (**Voice-over**)

▶ *Aoife's Memories*

Creating still images in groups

Before still image

- The children are asked to get into small groups of four or five. The teacher repeats the voice-over above. She then tells them that as a group they will be given some time to try to create an image of a moment from the past, which made Aoife determined that something would have to be done about the children. They are reminded that they need to listen carefully to each other while they are working, and that they can include any props which are available to them in the room (e.g. furniture, objects).

During still image

- While the children are working, the teacher should circulate around the room and assist them in terms of their understanding of the task in hand, and their attempts to assign roles within the group. She should also ask questions to provoke thinking and imagination. She should encourage them to try out their ideas physically *throughout* the process. She explains that she will soon be counting from ten to one, and that when she reaches one, the images should be frozen.

➤

After still image: sharing and reading images, learning to hold images

- The teacher asks the children to hold their images for about three seconds. She asks them to remember exactly what they are doing with their bodies and faces, and then asks them to relax.

- On the count of three the children resume their images, and while they are frozen the teacher asks them a number of questions to reflect upon, e.g. *What are you doing at this moment? What is your attitude towards the other people in the picture? What happened just before this moment? What do you think is going to happen next? What would you like to happen next?* (**Belief**)

- Again the children are asked to relax and it is explained to them that the next time they go into the image, they should try to have a look at all of the other images. This is because we want to find out *all* of the things that Aoife was remembering from her past. It is explained to them that they should try to stand in such a way that they can see the other images but would be ready to go in to their own image very quickly if asked.

- The teacher explains that she will now throw a 'spotlight' on to each of the groups in turn. She explains that she will do this by clicking her fingers over a particular group and by counting from three to one. When she reaches one, the group should resume its image while the other groups look on. Each group holds its image for only a few seconds as the spotlight moves around the room. (**Spotlighting**)

- The teacher engages the children in a general review of all images following the spotlighting exercise, e.g. *What kinds of memories did Aoife have? What did the images have in common? What kinds of feelings did you notice in the images?*

▶ *Reading images in more detail (options)*

During this type of reading, the teacher is trying to help the children to consider in more detail the potential motivations and meanings within each image. During the discussion, the teacher should also be conscious of opportunities which may help to focus on the themes or underlying questions of the drama. The sample questions which follow should help the children in their reading of still images.[5]

What words come to mind when you see this image? Who do you think is the central character in this image? What questions would you like to ask him/her if you had a chance? Are there any tensions (problems) in this image? Where do you see them? What might have caused them? What do you think happened just before this moment? What do you think will happen next?

Thought tracking: two approaches

1 To the group: *When I put my hand on this character's shoulder I would like you to tell me what you think is going on in his/her head?*

OR

2 To the characters in the picture: *In a few minutes I will put my hand on your shoulder and I would like you to share what you are thinking.*

> ▶ *Image of the ideal (optional) (fourth/fifth class)*

- Ideal image: Each group is asked to make changes to the above image to represent Aoife's ideal image of family life. The children could either be given time to work on this in their groups, or it could remain as a class activity by collectively sculpting changes to just one of the images. This means that one or more children would work as sculptors by physically moving the people in the image to reflect Aoife's ideal.[6] The children could then discuss the changes that could have taken place in the Lir household for Aoife's ideal image to be realised.

Possibilities for Progression

The two sessions described in detail to this point provide a way in to the drama and help to build context and investment. The following section outlines a variety of possibilities for progression.[7] However, in the end perhaps only a selection of such possibilities are likely to be used within a particular scheme of work. The choice of moments and the ways in which they might be combined will depend both on the children's interests and on the chosen thematic and dramatic focus of the scheme. The section on 'Structuring for Dramatic Experience', in Chapter 1 Planning and Facilitation, should be a helpful guide to the teacher in terms of facilitating the children's preferences for progression. A close examination of the other dramas in this book will also be helpful in this regard.

> ▶ *Exploring Aoife's Perspective*
>
> - The children have the opportunity to question Aoife in order to explore further her motivations and actions. (Hot seating, see Chapter 3, Teacher-in-role)
>
> - The children create the voices in Aoife's head on the night before the spell is cast and/or on the night after the spell has been cast. This idea can also be carried out with the whole class. In this case two lines are formed on either side of the character of Aoife, who hears the voices in her head as she walks between them (**Conscience alley**). This activity can also take place in small groups where one becomes Aoife (frozen or asleep) and the other two represent the voices (perhaps conflicting voices) in her head.
>
> - The spell: In groups the children focus on the casting of the spell using a devised text or script. (**Improvising with text and movement**, see p. 70)
>
> - Lir's dreams: The children create Lir's recurring dream of the children changing into swans through dance. (**Dance**, see p. 73)
>
>

▶ Exploring Lir's Perspective

- Inserting new tension: Aoife writes a letter to Lir three weeks after the spell has been cast. In her letter she explains that she has been unable to sleep since the terrible day she cast the spell on the children. She also informs him that she has been back to see the old woman in the hills who originally gave her the spell, and there is something she needs to talk to him about. Finally Aoife requests a meeting with him as soon as possible and begs him to agree to meet her. (**Tension**)

- The children advise Lir (teacher-in-role) about how he should deal with Aoife. The teacher, at least initially, takes an attitude of caution and fear in relation to the idea. (See Chapter 3, **Teacher-in-role**)

- The children explore the resulting meeting between Lir and Aoife through paired improvisation. Briefing: The children playing the role of Aoife are told to inform Lir that the old woman claims that the only way for the spell to be broken is for all of the Lir family to try to live together in the castle again. The children as Aoife must consider how they might persuade Lir to take such a risk. (See Chapter 4, **Paired improvisation**)

▶ The Journey of the Children of Lir

- Recreating the storm: The pupils then create a collaborative sound collage for one of the worst storms the swans encountered. (**Sound collage**)

Opportunities for Poetic Action

In the following sections three of the ideas above will be explained in more detail; they relate to the spell, the storm and the transformation of the children into swans through dance. The conventions and approaches associated with these ideas may have been alluded to in other sections of the book, but will now be illustrated in more detail. You may note that the approaches to recreating the spell and the storm in emphasis tend to encourage a more conscious manipulation of the art form. They might be referred to by Jonothan Neelands as examples of poetic action (Neelands, 2000, p. 6), in that they involve a particularly selective use of symbol, time and space to express and communicate meaning.[8]

▶ The Spell: Improvising with Text

- Working with the voice: The children are given the opportunity to recreate the words of Aoife's spell in groups. Based on a specific extract which is given to the children, each group focuses on how they might present a different section or line of the spell.[9] The teacher initiates a discussion on the various options available in advance, e.g. unison *v.* individual work; loud *v.* soft sections; high *v.* low sections; repetition and background noise.

- Additional dimensions: A variety of percussion instruments and movement can later be explored within this activity.

- The teacher spreads out a large circular blue sheet in the centre of the room, and asks the children in their groups to sit around the sheet (see p. 72). They are told that this sheet will represent Lake Derravaragh. Before each group presents its spell, the teacher guides the remaining children into role as Lir's children who are about to hear Aoife's fateful words. This can be done through guided imagery, e.g. *What has your day been like so far? What was your journey like? How did you travel? Who did you sit beside? What did you talk about? What did you see on your way?* (**Guided imagery**)

- The children, in groups, begin to present their spells to the other pupils. For maximum effect, in terms of atmosphere, each group presents its spell one directly after the other. (**Sharing**)

- The teacher helps the children to reflect on the experiential and aesthetic aspects of the activity above. *As the children of Lir how did you feel when Aoife began to call out the spell? Based on what you have seen and heard, what kind of mood do you think she was in? How did she show that mood? What kinds of things did people do with their bodies/voices to give this impression?* The teacher helps to draw the children's attention to variations in height level, use of voice, props and movement. She also asks them to consider the relationship between these effects and the meanings which they communicated. (**Reflection**)

▶ *The Storm: Sound Collage*

Specific background
In advance of the following activity, the children create a group/class mural highlighting the journey of the children of Lir across the waters of Ireland. It includes the landmarks and various sights which they passed, and highlights the most difficult sections of the journey for the children.

Recreating the storm through sound and movement
- The teacher asks the pupils to locate the worst storm the swans experienced on the class mural. *What, do you think, did the children see around them at this point in their journey? Do you think they would have encountered storms like this before? What signs would have helped them to recognise that a storm was approaching? What kinds of things would have provided shelter during this storm? What would they have done if they didn't find shelter?* (**Context**)

- The teacher helps the children to begin to see the possibilities for sound collage. *If we were to try to make the sounds of the storm in this room, how do you think we would do that? What could we use?* The children's answers may include variations on the use of voice, body and objects. (**Objects/props**)

→

- The teacher introduces a very large circular piece of coloured material (large enough to allow each child to hold a section on its circumference). The sheet is placed on the floor and the children are asked to sit around the edge of the sheet. They are told that this represents the section of their journey which was known to have some of the wildest and most difficult storms in Ireland. The teacher asks the children for ideas, instructions and demonstrations about how the whole class could use this sheet to represent the lake/sea during this storm, e.g. *the whole class could try to create the effect of waves by raising and dropping certain parts of the edge of the sheet; they could spin the sheet in a circular movement by moving around in a circle.*

- The group can agree on a piece of narration which would signal the beginning of the storm. Other signals can be agreed in advance with regard to the storm getting wilder and getting calmer. (**Sound collage**)

Sound collage: the storm.

◗ *Dance: Changing from Children to Swans*

The following dance, which allows the children to explore the transformation from children into swans, begins with an exercise which develops into a dance. The mirroring activity, which is central to the dance, provides a particular aesthetic form for exploration, which is loose enough to allow for a subsequent improvised and expressive response to ensue. The rationale for this type of approach will be explained in more detail in the second part of the chapter.

Mirroring experience (pairs)

The children are told that every night since the children disappeared, Lir experienced a recurring dream of their transformation into swans. The children are asked if they would like to be the children in Lir's dreams for a little while. They speculate on the length of time it took for the transformation to be complete along with the kinds of movements and shapes which they might have made with their bodies.

- The teacher leads the children in a stretching out of the main areas of the body: legs, arms, neck and back. This can be done as a copying exercise if the children need more guidance in this area. It can also be done with a musical accompaniment. (**Warm up**)

- Each child finds a partner. After a demonstration by the teacher with another pupil, or with her own hands, each child is asked to create a mirror with his partner. One partner is the leader, and one is the follower. The children should be encouraged to remain silent during this exercise, and to keep the symmetry as precise as possible between partners.[10] At all times the leader should be encouraged to challenge his partner, but not to make it impossible for him to maintain the synchronicity of the convention. The children can later swap roles so that the follower becomes the leader. (**Mirroring in pairs**)

- The children, still in pairs, are asked to stand behind one another, and to explore the same exercise from this position. Each child mirrors the movement of the child who is standing in front of him. The teacher can add music to enhance the experience. The children are encouraged to listen carefully to the music, and not to think too consciously about what the next movement will be. In this activity, the leadership is passed from one to the other, when the leader turns his body fully around to face in the direction of his partner. Because his partner is mirroring, he will also turn to face away from his partner, and will then become the leader. The children can later be encouraged to allow the leadership to pass from one to the other without having to be instructed to do so by the teacher. (**Changing leadership – adding music**)

Moving from exercise to dance (groups)
- Each pair now stands beside another pair, so that the class is now divided into groups of four. The children are once again asked to bring their attention to the moment in the story when the spell was cast. The teacher reminds the children of the variety of ways in which Aoife's spell was delivered (see p. 70). (**Context**)

→

- The children are now asked to prepare to go into movement again, and are reminded to follow their partners as before even though they are standing in a group.[11] This time they are asked, when they are moving, to be aware of how the children of Lir were feeling about what was happening to their bodies. It is emphasised that they do not necessarily have to recreate the exact movements of the swans, but to allow the feeling of the children at that time to be their most important guide.

- The teacher marks the beginning of the dance by taking on the role of Aoife and calling out the spell, using some of the ideas previously generated by the children. She then plays a new piece of appropriate music to accompany their work.

Dance: the transformation from children into swans

Sharing the dance

After a period of exploration, there are a number of ways in which the children can share their work if they wish to do so. Again it must be emphasised that when the children are sharing they are still improvising, and ultimately being led by their leader. It would be impossible and indeed undesirable for them to try to reproduce the work they have already created during the previous stage. As always it is a good idea to give the 'audience' in such an activity a purpose or a frame for the watching, so that they are included in the process rather than standing outside it.

Options for sharing

- The teacher could quietly ask three of the groups to rest while the others continue their movement. The children who are observing simultaneously create the sounds of the storm using voice and percussion. (**Sound collage**, see p. 71)

- The teacher can suggest more complex contributions from the 'audience' while the other half of the class is subsequently sharing their work.[12]

Examples:
   - The audience call out the spell as developed in the previous session before or during the movement piece.
   - The audience as Lir whisper the words of consolation that he calls out to them in his dreams.
   - The audience call out Aoife's responses as she begins to see the result of her actions unfolding in front of her. (**Conscience alley – adapted**)

- All of the groups engage in the movement exercise again, but this time they are conscious of the change from swans into people, rather than the initial change from people into swans. This could be particularly effective if the spell had been undone during the course of the drama.

Reflection on the above experience

- *Participants*
   - *How did it feel when you were the swans/when you were involved in that movement/dance? What did you hear around you? What effect did that have on you?*

- *Audience*
   - *What words came to mind when you were watching the swans?*
   - *How did Aoife react when she was watching them change into swans?*
   - *What did you notice about the way in which they moved? How did they use their bodies to create that effect?*

Devising a Performance from a Process Drama (Optional)

If the children and the teacher subsequently desire it, some of the moments from the previous process drama have the particular potential to be integrated into a more choreographed performance piece for a formal or informal gathering. The following ideas, which represent a development of moments from the previous process drama, will inevitably need to be added to and adapted during the rehearsal period, as is the case with all creative activity. As you will notice, one of the advantages of deriving a performance from process-based activity is that a sense of communal enterprise is maintained throughout. Most of the moments below can be performed by groups of children or by the whole class group. [13]

- The narration of the story by Machaomog: This could be devised by a child or group of children. There are many options available in terms of how this narration could be integrated with the ideas below. (**Narration**, see p. 64)

- Projected images of sections of the story and/or more abstract Celtic images can be used for background. Also the large sheet used for the Sea of Moyle could be used at various stages of the performance. (**Props**, see p. 63)

- The sound collage of the storm using material, voice, physical and musical props could be included and performed by a small group or the whole class. (**Sound collage**, see p. 71)

- The children could perform the spell through variations in sound and movement. (**Playing with text**, see p. 70)

- The dance sequence of the change from children to swans: After a period of improvisation, the children could identify a more precise order in terms of leadership that could be stated. Otherwise, much of the movement can remain improvisational. (**Dance, music**, see p. 73)

- Depending on the resources of the school, the use of simple lighting could prove extremely effective in bringing the atmosphere of the story to the fore. As is the case with the use of props and music above, it is most important that the children are involved in the decision-making with regard to implementing such ideas. (**Lighting**)

▶ Integration

Examples of ways in which this drama has been integrated with other subject areas:

Integration and *The Children of Lir*

SECTION OF *THE CHILDREN OF LIR* DRAMA	SUBJECT/STRAND	SKILLS
• Listening to Machaomog's story	English Strand: Receptiveness to language	Listening and responding to folktales.
• Creating the storm through sound	Music Strand: Composition Strand: Listening	Predicting and hypothesising in relation to 'unfinished' areas of the story. Creating abstract musical compositions to represent or respond to the natural environment.
• Creating a mural/ collage of the storm	Art Strand: Paint and colour; Fabric and fibre	Developing sensitivity to colour and tone, texture, line and shape.
• Performing the spell, playing with text	English Strand: Emotional and imaginative development through language	Empathising with characters. Language development – emotions, attitudes.
	SPHE Strand: Myself and others the nature of tension	Exploring and understanding the nature of tension.
	English Strand: Receptiveness to language causes and effects of actions	Exploring the relationship between the potential causes and effects of action.
	English Strand: Emotional and imaginative development through language	
• Movement – Changing from children into swans	Physical Education Strand: Dance	Developing a vocabulary for movement; developing creativity in movement.
• Making and responding to still images of Aoife's memories of her experience in the Lir household	Physical Education Strand: Dance	Developing a vocabulary for movement; developing creativity in movement.

PART TWO: WORKING PHYSICALLY IN DRAMA

> *The most important element of theatre is the human body.*
>
> (Boal, 1992)

> *The method of physical actions is the result of my whole life's work.*
>
> Stanislavsky (cited by Sonia Moore, 1976, p. 13)

> *Just as we convey messages and communicate with words, so can meaning and emotional feeling be conveyed through the body.*
>
> (Slade, 1995, p. 211)

Introduction

In many of the dramas in this book, you will notice that much attention is given to the children's physical engagement with the fiction at hand. This tendency involves a concern not merely to keep children's attention or to dissipate excess energy, but more importantly to address fundamental theatrical and educational principles inherent in the success of the drama itself. Boal's assertion above is representative of a long tradition within the theatre which views the body as an important signifier of meaning, medium of self-expression, and aesthetic visual form. Infamous directors such as Stanislavsky and Grotowski would claim that they have given their life's work to the practical exploration of the connection between physicality and character formation.

Directors and practitioners such as Augusto Boal and Bertolt Brecht have given particular attention to the ideological and political manifestations which emerge when actors, and non-actors, are asked to 'demonstrate' rather than talk about their responses to situations, concepts and images in real life. These directors have tended to base their practice on exploring the complex relationship between mind and body for theatrical purposes. The discussion in the remainder of this chapter will demonstrate that, apart from the development of a physical medium of expression in children, a very significant benefit of such exploration in the context of process drama is an increase in commitment to role and to the drama in general. This is partly due to the 'slowing down' of the drama, and the depth of exploration which such activity makes possible.

The centrality of the body has also been strongly advocated by educational theorists. The first chapter of this book outlines the importance of 'play' to the child's personal, physical, intellectual and artistic development. Piaget's discussion of the progression from practice to personal play in terms of its centrality to child development, is representative of a strongly held belief among educational practitioners in the importance of physical experimentation with and exploration of the material world. As teachers, we must embrace the challenge of addressing this desire and need in children for physicality, not only in the infant classroom but also throughout the primary school years. Throughout the drama continuum (from play to process drama to theatre) physical exploration finds its home in the context of a fiction. This means that children are initially motivated to engage with movement through some fictional need. In *The Children of Lir* drama the children explore character through mime, they explore Aoife's memories through still image, and they explore Lir's dreams through dance. It is our belief that children's ongoing exposure to such a variety of physical forms of expression and representation in their drama work has the effect of developing their general capacity for using the body as an artistic medium.

It follows from all of this that central to any drama programme is the opportunity to engage in activities and explorations which help children to develop their individual capacity to express themselves, to communicate, and to gain a better knowledge of self through the body. In summary, such activity provides children with an important access point to learning *about* and to learning *through* the art form of drama. In the sections below, a number of approaches to physical activity in educational drama will be discussed with reference to examples from *The Children of Lir* drama. These include:

- **Exercises and games**
- **Mime**
- **Still image**
- **Dance**

In each case a brief rationale will be given for such an approach, together with practical guidelines for its implementation. As in other chapters these guidelines will be discussed in terms of considerations before, during and after the experience. In all cases you will notice that not only is there is a lack of reliance on verbal language *per se*, but also there is a lack of reliance on a *shared* verbal language among the participants during such activity. This quality, which is particularly relevant to the multicultural context of many Irish classrooms, demonstrates once again the democratic nature of much dramatic activity. The exploration of ideas and emotions through the body also allows for a multiplicity of meanings to emerge within a given situation. This is because of the variety of interpretations which a more visual than verbal form affords.

Finally teachers should be reminded of the relationship between safety and participation which is central to all drama, and particularly relevant to physical exploration within drama. As children have little to 'hide behind' in such activity, the need for low focus activity, particularly in the early stages of such work, will be an important aspect to consider. Low focus activity refers to activity which is simultaneous and does not require the group to focus on individuals or small groups. (Poulter, 1987)

▶ *Exercises and Games*

> *In the body's battle with the world, the senses suffer. And we start to feel very little of what we touch, to listen to very little of what we hear, and to see very little of what we look at. We feel, listen and see according to our speciality; the body adapts itself to the job it has to do . . . In order for the body to be able to send out and receive all possible messages, it has to be reharmonised.*
>
> (Boal, 1995, p. 61)

Boal refers here to what is known as the mechanisation of the body. In our daily lives we accommodate our bodily movement to our routines. Boal would argue that a similar process also takes place in the mind. We see what we expect to see, we hear what we expect to hear and we respond in the way we usually respond to such information. In drama, we challenge and invade routines. We are asked to examine what seems ordinary with eyes that make it extraordinary. Whether within a fictional experience, or independent of it, an important task of the teacher is to reawaken within the child the potential of his body for expression, for exploration of place, time, character and self. This sometimes involves exercises which challenge children to explore a variety of ways of moving in terms of speed, height and manipulation of one's muscles, joints and skeletal framework.

We have found Augusto Boal's *Games for Actors and Non Actors* (1995) and Christine Poulter's *Playing the Game* (1987) particularly helpful in terms of providing examples and explanations of such exercises. In many cases, the exercises in these books are explained in the context of 'games' which are very effective in terms of simultaneously building safety and engaging children's interest in a drama. Many drama practitioners adapt these games and exercises to the fiction at hand. This is because while certain exercises in themselves are beneficial in terms of skill building, the lack of a fictional link to the drama can break the flow of the work leaving some children unfocused because of a perceived lack of purpose to the activity. In general we have found that once a fiction has been initiated, games and exercises, if required, should be linked to the fiction at hand. Exercises which may provide important skill-building opportunities, but are difficult to link with the drama, can take place before the drama begins or can be integrated with another subject area.

Examples of exercises for exploring movement

Bearing in mind the spontaneous nature of the dance activity which is suggested in the latter sections of *The Children of Lir* drama, the following preparatory exercises can be helpful to children who have little experience of dance. They can be employed or adapted within the fiction or outside of the fiction. During these exercises children stretch out the body, move at different speeds and height levels, explore different types of walks and so on. Throughout this work they are learning about their individual capacities within a new language, and subsequently develop a verbal vocabulary for movement. Such exercises should also help the children to move more freely and unselfconsciously when it is required.

Examples

- The children are asked to move around the space in different directions, and are encouraged to make pathways in and out between the other children as if they were moving through a maze. On the teacher's direction the children are asked to move at different speeds around the room. This can be developed into further challenge. *When I say 'fast', that means slow, when I say 'slow' that means fast!* (**Moving at different speeds**)

- The children are told that as they are moving around the room, they will be led by one body part e.g. left elbow, nose, right ear. They should become aware of how this imaginary pulling affects the way the rest of the body moves. (**Using the body in different ways**)

- The teacher guides the children on a journey through a variety of different environments e.g. forest, swamp, hot sand or deep water. The change in context should affect their movement. The children are reminded that at various stages of the journey, they will need to move at a high, low or middle level. (**Moving at different levels**)

  In pairs, or as a class group, the children discuss the kinds of movements they needed to make while they were on their journeys. (**Developing vocabulary for movement**)

Mime

The earliest origins of mime as an art form go back to the Greek Theatre of Dionysus in Athens, where everyday scenes were performed with elaborate gestures to audiences of ten thousand or more. In the Middle Ages the relationship between mime and mask was developed through the work of the *Commedia dell'Arte* in the market places of Italy. Mime also has its roots in the work of the early, silent film stars such as Chaplin and Keaton. The more theatre-specific approach to modern mime is represented in the very stylised work of Marcel Marceau, who was influenced by post-war artists Jean-Louis Barrault and Charles Dullin.

In the context of process drama however, children are engaged in mime activity less to convince an audience of a particular imitation of reality, than to immerse themselves more deeply in the fiction. In general, the use of mime in drama helps children to examine characters more deeply, or to immerse themselves in a new role. The rationale for this is that children will gain more in terms of belief and insight when they physically involve themselves in the doing of the smaller tasks of a character's day than by making detached and broad verbal speculations about what a character, job or perspective *seems* to be like. For example, in a drama about the *Titanic*, a child playing a crew member who has physically been involved in the building of the ship, will be more engaged on an emotional level when later challenged about the ship's design, than a child who has simply talked about such things in the abstract.

The physical preparation for the journeys in both the *Tom Crean* and *Winter's Dilemma* dramas serves a similar purpose. The use of mime provides a good basis for the making and reading of still images, and for other forms of movement activity such as dance. It is also particularly effective when working with young children not least because it is an activity within which children can work individually.

▶ Exploring Character and Role through Mime

Let us consider the example of how mime is used in *The Children of Lir* drama. In Session 3 of the drama, the children are engaged in a mime as the character of Aoife as she prepares for the day on which she plans to cast the spell. The main aim of this section of the drama is to begin to allow the children to explore the world from Aoife's perspective. As recommended previously, one way of doing this is to encourage the children to physically engage in the smaller activities of the earlier part of her day. This physical study of Aoife's preparation for the day, such as dressing herself or packing for the trip, may provide a more in-depth insight into her character and possible motivations than a rush to more all-embracing questions such as *Why did Aoife do it? How did she feel?* While these questions may indeed be asked at a later stage in the drama, the children will tend to approach them with more complexity if they have engaged in the experiential work above.

Some practitioners tend to use the term occupational mime to refer to the building of more generic roles in a drama (Toye and Prenderville, 2000). As discussed in Chapter 1, Planning and Facilitation, such roles may involve jobs or occupations which represent the basic framework of a small society. Much effort on the children's part goes into building the generic roles for such societies, e.g. farmers, teachers, bakers, builders, fishermen and spiritual leaders, so that they 'care' when the delicate framework upon which such communities rest is challenged. As we have seen, other generic roles which are helpful in process dramas are interviewers, researchers, investigators and explorers. Usually, the children will tend to be involved in the physical exploration of the specific tasks of such roles in the early stages of a drama. The following questions may help the teacher to support and initiate such exploration: *What do you do in the morning? What do you wear? How do you dress? How do you work? What tools and materials do you use? How exactly do you use them? What do you do in the evenings?*

▶ Practical Guidelines for Facilitating Mime

The following are some of the key practical guidelines which were inherent in the approach to mime within *The Children of Lir* drama, and which we have found useful in general. Overall it is most important that the exploration is set up in such a way that children understand it to be an improvised process of discovery rather than an attempt to display sophisticated mime skills. Before a mime exploration begins, the children should be clear with regard to the context of the mime. (*Who are you? Where are you? When is this happening?*) It can also be helpful for children to establish an initial freeze (e.g. a freeze of Aoife asleep in bed), and to establish an agreed signal for the mime to begin. Sometimes a line of narration can be effective in addition to this signal, e.g. *As Aoife turned over in her bed, the plans for the day ahead began to come back into her mind, and she knew it was time to get ready*. Such initial preparation may be enough to provide an easy way into mime.

The main emphasis now is on the child's individual unplanned discovery. However, the very *subtle* use of teacher-in-role, or narration during the mime itself, can also serve to enhance or focus the work, particularly if the teacher feels it is becoming lost or repetitive. In the *Tom Crean* drama, the teacher went into role as the observing Captain Scott when the children as explorers were preparing for their journey to the South Pole. This gave them a concrete reminder of the purpose of their exploration. The following are examples of narration which can serve a similar purpose during a mime exploration. They can apply to a variety of roles and situations. For example:

- *It is now morning time; how does your day begin? It is now one o'clock, three o'clock, seven o'clock, eleven o'clock etc.*

- *After a while you decide to take a break and do something that is really special to you . . .*

- *Aoife decided to go to the cupboard and take out something she had been hiding for years.*

You will notice that each of these examples represents an invitation to move more deeply into role. They are also open-ended questions which do not require a verbal response.

Dance

While dance is officially contained within the physical education curriculum, it is also important to understand it as an art form in its own right, and one which can be very effectively integrated with drama. The limited history of dance in Irish schools reflects similar tensions to those we are familiar with in drama. The debate between a desired emphasis on process or product has been reflected in the various approaches to dance in schools, and represents similar concerns with the balance between aesthetic and personal development in drama. It is not within the scope of this book to chart the history and theoretical basis of this debate, or to give professional advice in the area of dance education, but to explore more deeply the particular use of dance in *The Children of Lir* drama. The principles which are shared between dance and drama, and those which are applicable to all aspects of movement in drama will be particularly emphasised.

In general, the approach to dance in this drama reflects Laban's view of the dancer as creator. As quoted above, Laban 'viewed the dancer as creator . . . and placed strong emphasis on personal expression: on spontaneous improvisation and experimentation; on creative activity as a means of evolving a style of dance which was "true" to the individual personality' (Haynes cited by Abbs, 1987, p. 149). Within dance programmes that are influenced by such a philosophy, the participant is initially introduced to an exercise or particular style of movement. This exercise or style is specifically chosen or created by the leader for its capacity to allow for subsequent personal adaptation, creativity and expression. As such it acts as an evocative and challenging launching-pad for improvisation. This contrasts with an approach to dance which emphasises the learning of very specific repeatable routines within which all aspects of movement are dictated in advance.

In *The Children of Lir* drama the transformation of the children into swans is explored through a dance which evolves out of a mirroring exercise. The use of this initial exercise has a number of benefits. Firstly it protects the children from both the self-consciousness and 'sloppiness' which can result from instructions which lack a framework, or access point to movement. Simultaneously the exercise is loose enough to allow them to play, to invent and to feel as they begin to transform the exercise into their own individual dance. In this regard it is important to discourage the children from making advance 'decisions' about how they will move. Instead their emotional connection with the movement itself, the fictional moment, and the music should enable them to inhabit and transform the initial movement sequence. Indeed you will notice that even during the sharing of the *Children of Lir* dance which is discussed on p. 73, the emphasis on spontaneous improvisation is still maintained. Despite this the inherent mirroring structure gives a satisfying impression of synchronicity and choreography to the observing pupils, and indeed to the participants themselves.

Still Image

> *In its most archaic sense, theatre is the capacity possessed by human beings – and not by animals – to observe themselves in action.*
>
> (Boal, 1995, p. *xxvi*)

> *Successful drama works through condensation and compression through process of 'aesthetic packing' which pupils can experience in a limited way in tableau.*
>
> (Fleming, 1994, p. 94)

The use of still images can be very effective within any drama, and can provide a very accessible medium for children in terms of meaning making and gaining a deeper knowledge of the art form. In short children are engaged in still images when they are creating a still representation of a particular moment in time. In drama education literature, such activity may also be referred to as 'tableau' or 'freeze frame'. For children it is helpful to explain this approach in terms of societal and artistic conventions with which they are already familiar e.g. photographs, sculptures and waxworks.

The main benefit of using still image in a drama is that it allows the children to slow down the narrative of the drama by focusing in an in-depth way on one particular moment. In *The Children of Lir* drama, the children are asked to create images of moments which affected Aoife's decision to put a spell on the children. During such an activity the children are required to explore ways in which to condense meaning using a range of non-verbal signals. As they experiment with the effect on meaning of subtle changes in position, gesture and eye contact between characters, they become familiar with the notion that theatre making is a more conscious exploration of how we communicate.

Children gain not only from the creation of images but also from the 'reading' of images. Reading an image involves a search for meaning based on the various signs, either intended or unintended, which are inherent in a representation. The focused activity of examining particular moments in time allows children to gain a deeper knowledge of the particular, while also gradually learning about universal themes and modes of communication. One of the most exiting things about reading images in the context of a group is that there will be many ways of interpreting an image because of the variety of perspectives present within a class group. Through her questioning of the image the teacher can encourage a deeper investigation of character, situation, motivation and relationship. It is important therefore that children do not interpret this exercise as a guessing game. The interpretations of the 'audience' are as important as the intentions of the group who created the image.

▶ Finding an Appropriate Frame for a Still Image

Deciding on a productive frame for a still image is a very important step for the teacher. The meaning of the word 'frame' in this context is analogous with the basic wooden framework for a house. This needs to be put in place before decisions are made about style, colour, contents of rooms, number of windows and so on. In the context of using a still image the frame is the fictional challenge or question which the teacher puts to the children to guide their exploration. This instruction should be loose enough to allow for a number of interpretations to emerge and yet focused enough to provide challenge and intrigue.

The frame for the still image work in *The Children of Lir* drama is to try *to create an image of a moment from the past, which made Aoife determined that something would have to be done about the children*. There are a number of important principles inherent in this frame which can be applied to the setting up of still images in general. Essentially the instruction provides an important balance between openness and focus.

- It is *open* to a number of options for exploration. For example, there are a variety of possible incidents the children could explore which could have prompted Aoife to such action.

- The tension between this moment and the children's knowledge of Aoife's future plans provides a *focus* for the activity. Children tend to lack motivation if the frame is *too* broad. For example, asking the children to create an image of 'Aoife and the children' is likely to be ineffective in terms of both engaging and challenging the children. This is because there is too little consideration of *when* in the story this should take place or what the *purpose* might be for exploring such a moment. The addition of such considerations within the initial instruction is likely to greatly improve the quality of the exploration.

- It implies *action* of some kind. Some teachers fall into the trap of asking children to create images of emotional *reactions* to events, e.g. *Create an image of Lir's reaction to the disappearance of the children*. Images which result from such instructions can often be superficial; as participants tend to feel the requirement to portray stereotypical and exaggerated facial expressions to represent emotions such as sadness, anger or happiness. This is because of the lack of awareness of potential for action in the original instruction. They will also be at a loss to know what to do with their bodies.

  The following example from the Tom Crean drama also demonstrates that moments of high emotional content are often best explored through focus on some functional activity. At a certain point in the journey, the children are told that Captain Scott will not be able to take all of the crew on to the next stage. They are told that he will therefore be observing their work as crew members so that he can make an informed decision about who will continue and who will return home. The children subsequently create images of their efforts as explorers at this particular time. Such an image of the crew practising and preparing for their journey is likely to be more effective emotionally than asking the children to create an image of the crew's reaction when they hear that some of them will be sent home. This example gives more opportunity for a 'felt' emotional response to evolve organically out of action than would a request for an immediate demonstration of emotion.

The following are further examples of the frames for still images which are suggested in this book:

- The children are asked to create the activities of the inhabitants of the forest during a year with no winter. (*Winter's Dilemma*)

- The children are asked to create photographs of difficult moments for the villagers on the journey to visit Winter's den. (*Winter's Dilemma*)

- The children are asked to create the construction of a sculpture for the museum to commemorate Tom Crean. (*Tom Crean*)

▶ Still Image: Practical Guidelines

The following summarises useful ideas for facilitating still images in the classroom. It will be important for the teacher to adapt them to the requirements of a particular situation or moment in the drama. They mainly relate to images which are created by children in groups, but they could be adapted to images created by individuals or pairs.

Before still image
- *Explaining still image (options)*
    - Analogy: The use of analogies mentioned above e.g. photographs, sculpture.
    - Mime: The children are asked to freeze in the middle of a mime exploration.
    - Demonstration: The teacher demonstrates a still image for the children.
    - Sculpting: The teacher can 'sculpt' a child into an image, and visa versa. The person who is being sculpted is like a piece of moist clay, and his body must respond to the non-verbal directions of the sculptor.

- *Framing the image:* The children are given an instruction which provides a fictional and thematic focus for the activity. (See previous section)

- *Identifying the context:* The children will need to be clear about the *who, where* and *when* of the moment before beginning their exploration.
    - Who will be in the image?
    - Where exactly will it take place?
    - When is it taking place?

During still image

- *Monitoring and probing:* The teacher's task while the children are working is to ensure that there is clarity about what has been asked, and to use questions which will help them to focus, e.g. *Does everybody know who they are going to be in the image? What would you like to say about the relationships between the people? How are you going to show that in the image? Will you need any props?*

- *Giving tasks to groups who have finished early:* Such tasks can include preparing captions for the image, developing one line of dialogue for each character, or creating another image to represent the previous moment or moment to follow.

After still image

The following approach invites children to operate as an 'audience' to each other's work. However, the traditional notion of how an audience should operate is challenged in that a very participative and active response is promoted. The process of sharing involves a communal search for meaning.

- *Remembering and holding images:* The teacher can assist the children in this task by asking them to hold the image for a number of seconds, to relax and to then resume the image. This also has the advantage of dissipating giddy energy that can be present when children are inexperienced or not fully engaged. It is also helpful to their concentration to ask them to focus their eyes on a certain point while frozen in the image.

The following are examples of questions which can be put to the children while the images are frozen, in order to deepen their engagement with character and situation. They do not require a verbal response.

- *What are you doing at this moment?*
- *What is your attitude towards the other people in the image?*
- *What has happened just before this moment?*
- *What do you think is going to happen next?*
- *What would you like to happen next?*
- *How would that be possible?*

- *Reading of images (verbal):* This consists of a more in-depth reading of each image with the help of probing questions from the teacher. During this type of reading, the teacher is trying to help the children who are reading the image to consider its motivations and potential meanings in more detail, particularly as they relate to the theme or focus of the overall drama. The children in the image will be able to hold their positions for a limited amount of time only, so it can be a good idea to have a new focus for the reading of each new image e.g. focus on a different character, or use a new strategy. (**Sculpting, thought tracking**)

➡

Possible avenues for exploration

- *What words come to mind when you see this image?*
- *Who do you think is the central character in this image?*
- *What questions would you like to ask him/her if you had a chance?*
- *Which characters seem to relate well to each other/to be good friends?*
- *Are there any tension/problems in this image?*
- *Where do you see them?*
- *What might have caused them?*
- *How is X feeling about Y?*
- *What do you think happened just before this moment?*
- *What do you think will happen next?*
- *If you had to put a title/caption on this image, what would it be?*
- *Compare and contrast two images that represent the same moment.*

Reading images through drama conventions

Images can also be read through the use of drama conventions. The conventions of spotlighting, thought tracking, sculpting, and sound collage are explained in the next section.

❱ *Drama Conventions Associated with Reading Images*

Spotlighting

Spotlighting is a useful technique to adopt when working with a group who find it difficult to hold and focus on images in a more in-depth way and for a more extended period of time. As demonstrated in *The Children of Lir* drama, the children focus their attention on one group at a time for just a few seconds. It can be effective to use music as a background for these images. Sometimes the music can provide an effective contrast with the content of the images. For example, a spotlighting activity based on images of war can be accompanied by a calm classical melody. Children in senior classes can suggest ideas with regard to the choice of this music.

Thought tracking

The group speculate about the thoughts of one or more of the characters in the image. Alternatively one or more characters volunteer their thoughts at the request of the group. The second option can be very helpful, if the class are finding the image difficult to read. It can also be interesting, in both cases, to examine the potential contrast between what characters are saying and what characters are thinking. This can be done through the convention of voices in the head, which means that a child from the group stands behind a character in the image and gives his/her real thoughts.

Changing the image through sculpting

When changing the image through sculpting, a child or group is asked to alter the image through physical manipulation. The person who is being sculpted is like a piece of moist clay, and his body must respond to the non-verbal directions of the sculptor. The focus for the sculptor(s) could include the following:

- Sculpt the moment before this moment.
- Sculpt the moment after this moment.
- Change the image so that it presents a more ideal or better situation for the characters e.g. Aoife's ideal of family life.

Sound collage

One group, or the class, is asked to spontaneously create a sound collage for the image which is being read. This can include verbal statements representing any character in the image, or non-verbal sounds that seem to be suggested by the environment of the image. This exciting activity will inevitably involve the overlap of voices and ideas, which makes for an interesting and often very honest response to the piece.

Footnotes

1   The images and storyline used in the planning of this drama were based on the version of the story in *The Names upon the Harp* (Heaney, 2000). It is strongly recommended that you refer to this or to another official version of the story in your planning.
2   P.J. Lynch's images in *The Names upon the Harp* (Heaney, 2000) were particularly effective in the classroom.
3   'Sculpting' could also be combined with this activity. One child sculpts the other as if he were a piece of clay by moving the various parts of his body into position.
4   Flow – the smooth development from one image into another.
5   More examples of questions are given in the second part of the chapter. It should be remembered that children can only hold and read an image for a limited period of time. Therefore, not *all* questions can be asked of all images!
6   Differences between the first image and second image can also be discussed. Depending on the content of these images, older classes could also explore, through images, the contrast between Lir's and Aoife's ideal of family life.
7   The compilation of such ideas during the planning process is sometimes referred to as brainstorming. The identification of a variety of possibilities for progression can be very helpful when a teacher becomes more experienced at working 'on her feet'. Such preparation will help to negotiate the desires of the children with the thematic focus of the work during improvised activity.
8   See Chapter 1 Planning and Facilitation for further discussion of different types of action in drama.
9   Heaney's version of the spell (Heaney, 2000, p. 22) is presented in the appendix of this book. Alternatively, the words of the spell can be created or adapted by the teacher to suit the level of the children. Older children may be able to create their own version of the spell in groups.
10   It is important that the children move slowly during this activity. In this regard it can be helpful to begin with mirroring one hand only and then adding further movement.

11   While we found that it was easier for third class children to share leadership in pairs, older or more experienced children may be able to pass the leadership among the group of four by placing themselves in a diamond shape at the beginning of the dance. As with the original idea they initially stand behind one leader and follow his movements and leadership is subsequently passed from one child to another.

12   See the discussion of *audience* in process drama in the second part of this chapter.

13   See Chapter 6 on *Using Script as a Stimulus for Drama* for a more detailed discussion of the issue of performance in the primary school.

THE EXPLORATIONS OF TOM CREAN

© *Royal Geographical Society*

PART ONE

*A Drama Based on the Explorations of Tom Crean
(Fifth/Sixth Class)*

PART TWO

Improvisation

PART ONE: A DRAMA BASED ON THE EXPLORATIONS OF TOM CREAN

Background for Teacher

The *Tom Crean* drama centres on investigating the influence that Tom Crean had on Antarctic exploration in the last century and especially on his contribution to the *Terra Nova* expedition. Tom Crean took part in three polar expeditions: *Discovery* (1901), *Terra Nova* (1910) and *Endurance* (1914). Robert Falcon Scott captained the first two expeditions. Ernest Shackleton captained the third expedition.

The children are placed in role at the beginning of this drama as researchers for the National Museum of Ireland with responsibility for investigating Tom Crean's involvement in polar exploration. Their task will later involve exploring and representing key incidents from his life. The children are first introduced to Robert Scott the captain of the *Terra Nova* expedition, and they investigate how to attract funding and recruit an expert crew. This follows an exploration of Tom Crean's background as a child in Annascaul in Co. Kerry, an experience which influenced his ambition to reach the South Pole.

The remainder of the drama explores Tom Crean's involvement in polar exploration and investigates what might have happened after he was selected to be among the final seven to reach the Pole. Unfortunately when Scott reduced this number to four at approximately 150 miles from the South Pole, Crean was left with no choice but to return to base camp. Scott decided on this course of action as he felt he had chosen too many men to accompany him on the last leg of the journey. He hoped this decision would prevent his competitor (Amundsen) from reaching the South Pole before him.

This drama uses the story of Tom Crean as a way of enabling children to explore connections between dreams and ambitions, and asks whether it is possible to realise all our dreams. It also investigates ways in which one's dreams might be challenged. The notion of inventing and reinventing one's dreams as life progresses and the value of recognising small achievements which may be inadvertently realised is also brought to the fore. The children are also led to examine what it means to be a hero.

As improvisation is used throughout this chapter, Part Two outlines the underlying knowledge and skills necessary to the implementation of improvisation in process drama. Essentially, improvisation enables participants to make new discoveries about characters and situations by stepping into the character's world and exploring the world from his or her perspective.[1]

▶ *Classroom Sessions*

- *Session 1: The Context; Exploring Antarctica*
- *Session 2: Scott Prepares for the Expedition*
- *Session 3: Meeting Tom Crean*
- *Session 4: Reaching Antarctica*
- *Session 5: Scott Encounters Problems in Antarctica*
- *Session 6: Emergency Return to Base Camp*
- *Session 7: Remembering Crean*

Seven sessions approximately (45 minutes to 1 hour each)

Session 1: Exploring Antarctica

▶ Background Information: Examining a Mysterious File

- The children are contracted into the fiction (see p. 21).

- Place Appendix 2 in an envelope and explain to the children that this information was taken from the National Archives library in Dublin in the recent past. Ask the children to work in pairs and discuss who might have an interest in this file and why. Elicit responses.

- Explain that the National Museum of Ireland has selected the children to research an Irish Antarctic explorer named Tom Crean, an individual who made a significant contribution to polar exploration. The museum hopes that the information gathered will be used to commemorate Crean. The children are told that they have been selected because of their excellent research skills.

- Elicit any prior knowledge that the children may have about polar exploration or exploration in general. Distribute the file information to the children (Appendix 2). Give the children time to explore the facts and revise the generated information (use map). Generate a discussion on Antarctica's relationship with other continents and countries. Examine physical features and placenames; focus on places such as the South Pole and the Ross Ice Shelf.

- The children are now told that as the commissioned researchers they will need to go back over the significant moments in Crean's involvement in polar exploration so that they will be able to decide which key moments should be included in the museum as part of the commemoration.

- The children are told that this drama will primarily focus on the *Terra Nova* expedition.

▶ Introducing Captain Scott

- The teacher now provides background information on Captain Scott.

- Introduce Robert Scott, the individual who captained two polar explorations; the first was *Discovery* (1901) and the second was *Terra Nova* (1910). Explain that Captain Scott, an Englishman, had a dream to be the first person to reach the South Pole. He made a noteworthy contribution to polar exploration. Despite not reaching his target during the first expedition, he still came within 410 miles of the South Pole and set a new furthest south record. After this experience he was determined not to give up his ambition of being the first person to reach the South Pole and therefore set about this quest in 1910.

Session 2: Scott Prepares for the Expedition

▶ *Advertising for the Crew*

- The children are asked to speculate about the kinds of expertise, skills and qualities which Scott might be seeking from a crew member in order to ensure success on his expedition.

- Firstly they are asked to imagine the advertisement Scott might have created to gather this expert crew, and secondly where he might have placed this advertisement. The children are placed in groups of three to compose the advertisement or poster which Scott might have used to recruit an able crew. Remind the children that Scott needed to make this advertisement as attractive as possible as he was aware that there were few monetary benefits to be gained from this trip. Generate a discussion on strategies which might best enhance this advertisement e.g. use of exaggeration, persuasive language. (**Link with media studies**).

▶ *Seeking Funding: Whole Class Improvisation*

Preparing for improvisation
- The children are told that Scott still had to overcome one significant challenge before he could go to the South Pole; he needed to get substantial funding. Question the children about who Scott might go to for funding. If the children do not suggest it, they are told that Scott approached a government official and had a meeting with him in his office.

- The children are told that they are going to get an opportunity in a few moments, to explore what happened when Scott and the government official met.

- The class are divided into two groups. One half of the class is placed in role as Captain Scott and the other half in role as the government official. Each of these two groups is further divided into three or four smaller groups. These small groups will ensure that all the children are given an opportunity to speak.

- The children are then informed that both the government official and Scott recognised that they had to do some research before this important meeting. The Scott group(s) are asked to come up with arguments in favour of getting funding and the government official group(s) are asked to consider challenging questions they would like to ask Scott during the meeting.

Briefing Scott
- While the Scott group are preparing for the meeting by generating written ideas, the teacher informs them that Scott secretly sees this expedition as a route to promotion. (**Inserting dramatic tension**)

Briefing government official

- While the Scott group continue to prepare for the meeting, the teacher asks the remaining children in role as the government official questions such as:

  I want you to carefully consider what is at stake before the forthcoming meeting. Do you have any concerns about funding this expedition? I presume you are familiar with Scott's previous lack of success with the Discovery expedition? Are you worried about his credibility given that he didn't succeed the last time? What is at stake if he fails to make it this time? I also know this expedition could be very beneficial for England if he succeeds, I want you to think about how it might benefit England.

  Before you make your mind up you need to listen carefully to Crean's points for and against Scott's request. I think you need to make sure that this man has done his preparation, ask him tough questions. Spend some time now preparing the questions you will ask him. (Inserting dramatic tension)

- While the government official group discusses these issues, go back to the Scott group and distribute additional challenges to them. (**See Appendix 2**)

- As the children continue their preparation, the teacher can move around the classroom and monitor the children's commitment to the task.

Creating the meeting place

- Once the children have prepared for the meeting, their attention can now be drawn to the day the meeting took place. Enable the children to create an internal picture of the government official's office by closing their eyes and imagining the colours, sounds, odours, type of furniture, and general mood of the place. Elicit children's responses e.g. 'I see pictures of battle on the wall'. After a few moments, the children are asked to open their eyes and to discuss their imaginings. (**Guided imagery**)

- The information provided by the children is used to set up the physical office space. They are encouraged to set out the furniture for forthcoming meeting. (**Reading signs**)

Explaining the format of the meeting

- Explain to the children that two volunteers will represent Scott and the government official in the centre of the room. The remaining children will sit in a semi-circle around the two characters. Those sitting in the semi-circle will be asked to assume their respective roles and to continue the conversation once the meeting has been started. (**Whole group improvisation**)

- Request the government official to sit in a chair in the centre of the room. Discuss with the class how they think he might sit, experiment with different positions and explore what each position signifies.

- The children decide how Scott might enter the room; what his body language might be like and whether this posture represents his mental disposition in any way.

- With the children's help decide whether Scott or the government official (children in the centre) will open the meeting, how it might be opened and how the other person will instantly respond.

During improvisation: the meeting

- The children who are positioned in the centre of the circle are advised to use the decided sentence to begin the meeting. The teacher encourages those sitting around in the semi-circle to continue the discussion once it has started. They are informed that any child (including the child on the chair) can speak as the character they are representing, either to initiate or respond to comments from the other side. The children are reminded during the conversation that both characters need to put their best foot forward as there is a lot at stake.

- As the meeting progresses, the teacher can pause the meeting at any point and reinforce the tension of the moment by speaking to each group privately. For example:

  - Scott group
    How do you feel the meeting is going so far? Scott make sure to contribute all your ideas, you really need to get funding, you know what this means to your career?

  - Government official group
    How do you feel the meeting is going so far? Do you feel that you have challenged Scott in any way? Government official you need to challenge Scott more, you have to be sure this is a worthwhile expedition. There is a lot at stake for England if he doesn't succeed.

- When sufficient time has been spent debating the issue, the teacher discontinues the meeting by announcing that the government official has another meeting to attend. Ask the children to find a way of bringing the meeting to a close.

Reflection on improvisation

- The children are questioned out of role once the meeting has concluded. The following are examples of possible questions.
  - *Was that meeting easy or difficult for Scott?*
  - *What were the biggest challenges the government official presented to Scott?*
  - *Did Scott successfully defend himself?*
  - *Are there any additional points he could have mentioned?*

- Inform the class that the government official reflected on all of the issues raised in the meeting for many hours and decided to donate £20,000 towards the expedition, 50 per cent for exploration and 50 per cent for science.

- Finally question the children on whether they think the government made the correct decision in supporting the expedition?

Session 3: Meeting Tom Crean

▶ Exploring Crean's Early Background

- The children are told that they are now going to explore what the early childhood experiences of the Irish explorer Tom Crean might have been like. They are reminded that this is the individual who they have been commissioned to commemorate for the National Museum of Ireland.

- Background information: The children are told that Tom Crean from Annascaul, Co. Kerry was one of the crew who went with Scott to Antarctica with the intention of reaching the South Pole. They are reminded that he went with Scott on both the *Discovery* expedition and the *Terra Nova* expedition.

- Other background information: He was born on 20 July 1877; there were ten children in his family and he came from a farming background.

- Working in pairs the children write, draw or mime what they think a typical day in Tom Crean's life might have been like at the age of ten. They are asked to begin this account at 8am and to continue exploring his day at 11am, 1pm, 4pm, 6pm, and 7pm. Remind them to think about issues such as education, leisure activities and so on. (**Developing character**)

- Generate a discussion on the similarities and differences between lifestyles today and in the past. (**Link with geography**)

▶ The Fair in Annascaul

Preparing for improvisation
- The children are told that the people in the past had a special interest in the local fair which took place in Tom Crean's village of Annascaul, usually once a month. Elicit and discuss its function, the nature of the entertainment which took place there and the importance of trading.

- The children's attention is now drawn to a significant experience Tom had when he visited the fair with his uncle. He was approximately ten years old. As Tom's dad could not go to the fair on this particular occasion he asked his brother to sell and buy some cattle for him. Tom's father had great respect for his brother's farming knowledge.

- Divide the class into pairs (A's and B's). Explain that in a moment the A's will become Tom and that the B's will become Tom's uncle, in order to imagine a day at the fair.[2]

➡

- In role, the children are now asked to close their eyes and to imagine that they have just arrived at the fair, ask them to imagine what they can see, hear, smell and to look and see at what is happening around them. (**Guided imagery**)

- While the children are visualising this moment narrate the following:

  When Tom and his uncle arrived at the fair they stopped and looked at the different entertainment stalls. The jugglers and musicians captured their initial attention. After a while Tom's uncle decided to focus his energies on selling the cattle he brought to the fair. He was hopeful that he could purchase some good replacement cattle.

  Tom was just about to accompany his uncle to the cattle area when he noticed a group of people gathering on a street corner close by. Filled with curiosity, he wandered over and was delighted when he realised a storyteller was setting up his stall. As Tom loved stories and especially those which dealt with faraway places, he decided to stay. He was captivated by what he heard and couldn't believe such places actually existed. He almost went into a trance as he imagined each place. While he was doing this, his uncle got on with the selling and buying of cattle for Tom's father.

- The children are told that in a few moments they are going to get an opportunity to find out what the conversation was like between Tom and his uncle on their way home that evening.

- The children are prepared to step into role aided by the teacher before the improvisation (**briefing**). This can be carried out at the back of the classroom or outside the door. While Crean is being briefed those in role as Tom's uncle are asked to make a price list of the cattle and other items he sold and bought that day. (**Integration**)

Briefing Crean

- The Crean group is briefed in the following way:

  What did you do today? Did you enjoy listening to the storytellers? Why? What kinds of things did they talk about? Why have you such an interest in stories about travelling? Would you like to go travelling some day? Was your uncle with you when you were listening to the stories? What was he doing? I want you to think about the specific places and adventures you heard about as I know you will want to tell your uncle all about them. It might be helpful if you put some of your ideas on paper as I know you have lots of ideas in your head. I believe your uncle will be coming to take you home soon. After he has had a chance to talk about his day make sure and tell him all about your exciting day and the way the storyteller has inspired your ideas about travelling in the future.

Briefing Tom's uncle

- While Crean considers the stories he heard that day, his uncle is taken aside and the following discussion takes place with him:

→

Did you enjoy your day? Were you happy with your purchases? What did you buy? Was Tom with you? What was he doing? Why didn't he come with you? How do you feel about this? I know his father hoped that he would pick up some farming tips from you today and I believe he would like him to help out more at home in the future. Perhaps you can encourage him to come along with you the next time instead of listening to storytellers. As you are very close with Tom you need to find a gentle way of convincing him.

- The children are asked to join up with their improvisation partner and begin the conversation which might have taken place between the characters. Encourage the children to walk around the classroom as they communicate with each other.

During the improvisation

- While the children are working in pairs the teacher monitors the improvisations in an effort to see whether they are committed to their roles (belief). It may be helpful to pause the improvisation after a few minutes and ask the children to come out of role and to think privately about the following questions:
  - *How are you feeling about the way the conversation is going?*
  - *Which aspect are you happy with?*
  - *Are you achieving what you set out to achieve, or is your partner changing your opinion in any way?* (***Character motivation***)
  - *Are you happy with your ability to take on this role?*
  - *If not do you need to make any changes?*

- After a few moments enable the children to resume the conversation in role.

- When an appropriate amount of time has elapsed, the teacher will need to consider ways of concluding the improvisation e.g. teacher-in-role as Tom's mother or father can announce, *Welcome back Tom, I hope you had a good day, I am looking forward to hearing all about it.*

After improvisation

- The children are asked to come out of role. They will now get an opportunity to discuss the content of the improvisation with their partner. Below are examples of questions that could be asked.

Content questions

- *How might the characters be feeling after they returned home?*
- *Were there any clashes between Tom's dreams and his family's ambitions for him?*
- *How did the characters react when they were faced with the challenge of having different future dreams?*
- *Were Crean's dreams at odds in any way with the prevailing beliefs about the way you should live your life at that time?*

→

Drama questions (form)

- *Were you happy with your ability to take on the role?*
- *Were there any aspects which were difficult?*

Narrative link

The teacher can prepare and share a newspaper heading from the *Annascaul News* with the children which informs them that Crean went on to join the British navy at the age of fifteen and subsequently was chosen to go on three expeditions to the South Pole.

Paired improvisation: Crean and his uncle return from the fair.

Session 4: Reaching Antarctica

> ### ▶ *Background to Reaching Antarctica*
>
> The teacher continues to read information from the *Annascaul News*:
>
> *Crean's first expedition was on board* Discovery *(1904). The second expedition took place six years later in July 1910 on board the* Terra Nova. *Scott requested that Crean would go on both expeditions. Scott especially wanted Crean to go on the second expedition as Crean had a wealth of polar experience at that stage. Before Scott departed for New Zealand, he encountered his first challenge when he received a telegram from Amundsen – a Scandinavian explorer – stating that he had already begun the quest of conquering the South Pole. Scott understood the gravity of this news and as a result was beginning to feel the pressure. However, he was determined not to allow Amundsen to defeat him and as a result promptly departed for New Zealand. He arrived in Antarctica on 6 January 1910. He set up base camp immediately at Cape Evans.*
>
> ### Preparation for the South Pole
> - Revise the profile and purpose of the crew: job descriptions, roles, duties and so on. (Refer to advertisements prepared in Session 2.)
>
> - The children are told that they will now be placed in role as crew members. They are asked to close their eyes and imagine that they have just arrived in Antarctica. They are asked to visualise and imagine the colours, sounds, feelings the crew might have experienced. Elicit responses. **(Guided imagery)**
>
> - The children are told that a hut was erected at Cape Evans and that all the resources were placed there.
>
> - In role as Scott the teacher explains the following:
>   *We are here in Antarctica a day, and we need to begin avid preparations for the long and arduous journey ahead of us. I need to tell you now that you will not all be going to the Pole with me, as it would prove unsuccessful. I therefore need to confine the number that will go with me to seven. Despite this, you must remember that our success depends on each crew member's effort. Our first important task will involve depositing food supplies along the route to the Pole for the returning party. Remember, this is essential as it is a 1,800-mile journey to the Pole and the men will need food on their return route. To help me decide whom I will choose I will observe each man's commitment over the forthcoming days.*
>
> ### Preparing for improvisation
> - Question the children about what food supplies might be needed for the returning party. Tell the children that Captain Scott divided the crew into working groups of four to prepare to deposit supplies. Ask the children to discuss the following in their groups of four: ➤

- *What mode of transport will your group use: dogs, ponies, motor tractors or sleighs?*
- *What resources will be needed?*
- *As all resources were initially stored in the hut, what is the best way of loading these items?*
- *What potential problems might be encountered while you are travelling?*
- *How will you prepare for these challenges?*

- As a further way of preparing the children to enter this improvisation, the children are asked to silently become aware of how they are feeling at this time given the pressure that they are under. Also, what impressions would they like to give as they are working? (**Character motivation**)

- The children are requested to mime and discuss the organisation and loading of the required resources. They are then asked to begin the journey once they have decided how to effectively use each member of their group. They are reminded that Scott (teacher-in-role) will be paying careful attention to their ability to co-operate under pressure. (**Small group improvisation**)

During improvisation

- Once it is felt that the children have been given a chance to invest in the situation, pause the improvisation. Ask the children to consider a problem which might have developed as the men were progressing along their route. This problem can be agreed by the group in advance of the improvisation, or the problem may evolve during the improvisation. (It will not be decided in advance.)[3]

- Further pause the improvisation after a few moments and ask the children to privately consider their characters' feelings and attitudes and the way these feelings might be affecting their relationship with the other members of the team. (**Reflection**)

- Encourage the children to continue the improvisation. The teacher-in-role as Scott can build further tension by moving around the space and openly saying: *I must closely observe the crew as I have a very difficult decision to make, I wonder who will I choose.*

After improvisation

- **Option 1:** The children discuss the content of the improvisation in pairs and share the observation with the teacher.

- **Option 2:** When sufficient time has been given to each group, ask the children to go back and pick a significant piece of dialogue which emerged among their group during the improvisation. They could be encouraged to choose a moment which depicts a key moment of tension. Give the children a chance to rehearse this moment by repeating it a few times.

- Once the groups have had a chance to rehearse their improvisations, one group can be selected to share its improvisation with the rest of the class. The remainder of the class will become observers. Their task will involve analysing the nature of the relationship which existed between the men and

➡

Chapter 5 THE EXPLORATIONS OF TOM CREAN

the strategies used by the group to impart meaning e.g. use of gesture, voice, eye contact and pause. Another group can share their chosen improvisation with the rest of the class once this group is finished.

- Following the sharing process, the children are told that after much deliberation, Scott selected Crean to go to the South Pole along with Lashly, Teddy Evans, Bowers, Wilson, Oates and Taff Evans.

- The children are informed that each man was told the news in private. Crean's reaction after receiving the news can be explored by placing an empty chair at the top of the class and telling the children that Crean sat in this chair as he pondered on the news. Elicit all the thoughts which might be going through his head at this time. Explore different reactions e.g. positive thoughts and any apprehensive thoughts which he may have had.

Improvisation: the crew working together to load the sleigh

The passing of time

As the evenings were devoted to recreational time, each man used this time in a special way. Options:

- Find a corner in the room and mime a special activity Scott might have engaged in during the evening.

- Crean's diary: Crean decided to catch up on his diary, as he had not written it since he came to Antarctica.

- Select key moments from the expedition that Pointing, the photographer, could have chosen for his album. Children could create still images of the significant photos which he selected.

Session 5: Scott Encounters Problems in Antarctica

Scott reduces his crew

- Another edition of the *Annascaul News* is shared with the children.
  Scott and his seven men made headway towards reaching the South Pole. They man-hauled everything. However, at approximately 150 miles from the Pole, Scott regretfully noticed that the men were beginning to slow down. Therefore, he made a prompt decision to reduce the number of the crew and regretfully had to inform those who would have to return and those who would continue to the Pole. He knew he had to do this immediately, as time was not on his side. All the men gradually became aware that this had to be done and as a result, waited nervously to discover their fates.

Preparation before improvisation

- The children are told that in a moment they will get a chance to discover Crean's future. To enable them to experience this moment they are divided into pairs, A and B. The children are told that all the A's will become Scott and the B's Crean.

- All the children who are in role as Crean are advised to set up their tents in preparation for the forthcoming meeting. Encourage them to make use of resources available in the classroom e.g. chairs, bags and tables.

Briefing Scott

- While the Crean group are preparing their tents, all the Scotts are gathered together and are informed that Scott has decided not to bring Crean to the South Pole. The children are also told that Scott was not looking forward to breaking the bad news to Crean, as he had developed a very close and respectful relationship with him over the years. He was also aware that Crean had a strong desire to reach the Pole. The children are asked to consider ways in which he might impart the news – should it be delivered in a formal or informal manner?

- The Scott group are also informed that Crean's tent was full of smoke when he entered it and that the incoming wind caused Crean to cough. They are told that Scott seized this opportunity and began the conversation with, *You've got a bad cold there Crean*. However, he knew he had to be ready with another reason as Crean may not accept this as a suitable excuse. The children are asked to consider other ways he might break the news.

Briefing Crean

- The Crean group are informed that Crean smoked his pipe while he waited to receive the news, he anxiously pondered on his future as he knew his lifelong dream could be shattered in an instant. The teacher asks him about how he will react if the news goes against him; will he complacently accept it or will he defend himself? They are also told that a puff of smoke caused Crean to cough once Scott entered the tent. Ask the children to practise this cough once.

- Before the improvisation begins request each group to do their best to imagine the situation and to speak as if they are the characters at this moment in time.

During improvisation

- The teacher monitors and evaluates the children's ability to improvise. (**Assessment**)

- After a few minutes, stop the improvisation and establish through whole class questioning if the characters are happy with the way the meeting is progressing.

- When an appropriate amount of time has elapsed consider ways in which the improvisation might be closed, e.g. *Scott needs to move on and deliver news to other members of the team so he must depart shortly.*

After improvisation

Question the children out of role e.g.
- *How did Crean feel after the meeting with Scott?*
- *Did Scott deliver the news in an appropriate way?*
- *Could he have done anything differently?*

▶ *Optional Stage: Sharing Improvisation*

Examining the subtext (unspoken dialogue)

- Tell the children that they are now going to examine the conversation which took place between Crean and Scott by picking out a significant piece of dialogue from the previous improvisation. Ask each pair (Scott and Crean) to select approximately three to four sentences from the conversation. Advise them to select a moment of tension between the two characters.

- Once this has been decided ask the children to rehearse this exchange again.

- The children are now told that the characters' unspoken thoughts at this time will be examined.

The process

- Instruct each pair to join up with another pair. One pair is instructed to stand behind the other pair. While one pair shares their chosen piece of dialogue with the other pair, the other pair are instructed to silently consider what they think the characters' unspoken thoughts might be at this time.

- Once the children have decided on the characters' unspoken thoughts, they can be asked to stand behind the group and to voice these thoughts aloud as the group repeat the dialogue. Reverse the process so that the pair working on the subtext can now become Crean and Scott.

- When each pair has practised they can be given an opportunity to share their piece with the rest of the class. (Optional)

Still image: Tom Crean helping his family on the farm (before departure)

Session 6: Emergency Return to Base Camp

- The children are informed that Crean, Evans and Lashly were asked to return to base camp. They are told that they were given enough rations to last the return journey. Once they had packed up their belongings, they began retracing their steps to base camp. Spirits were low and they also knew that the journey ahead would not be easy.

- The children are divided into groups of three and asked to decide which character they would like to assume (Crean, Evans or Lashly). They are told that they will be improvising the men's reaction to Scott's news. They are reminded to privately consider the following reflective questions before they begin improvising: *How are you feeling? What is the mood like between the men?*

- Give the children an opportunity to begin improvising this situation.

- After the children have been given sufficient opportunity to engage with the early stages of the men's return journey, pause the improvisation and inform them that not long after they had commenced their journey tragedy struck as Evans developed scurvy. Unfortunately his condition rapidly deteriorated, and as a result the men were therefore confronted with another problem.

- The children are told that in a few moments they are going to demonstrate Evan's deterioration using non-verbal means. To do this they are asked to create a sequence of still images. Request the children to repeat each image using a slow motion movement and to consider how to smoothly move from one image to the other. If desired, verbal improvisation could be added to the sequence once children have worked on the non-verbal sequence.

- After the children have been given a chance to explore the dilemma the men were faced with, discuss a suitable course of action they could take. The teacher tells the children that she has a letter which Evans subsequently wrote to his family about this experience.

A few months later
- The following information can be written in the format of a letter: Crean volunteered to rescue his colleague Evans by returning to base camp to seek help, while Lashly stayed with Evans. This journey was thirty-five miles in length and Crean had only three biscuits and two pieces of chocolate to sustain him and was without sleeping gear. Crean succeeded in reaching base camp to get help, and therefore saved Evans's life. At the same time, Scott's party reached the Pole to discover that Amundsen had already beaten them. Weak from exhaustion, hunger and extreme cold, Scott died on the return journey.

- The children are informed that Crean returned to England with very mixed feelings after this episode.

- The following reflective questions can be used to help direct a discussion on the overall theme of the drama.
    - *Why did Crean have mixed feelings upon his return to England?*
    - *Did Crean accomplish anything?*
    - *Do you think the expedition was worth it?*
    - *What should he do now?*
    - *Is it worth striving for something else?*
    - *Have you ever encountered obstacles which hindered you from achieving your goals?*
    - *What obstacles might stop us from reaching our goals in life?*

Session 7: Remembering Crean

- This session is linked with Session 1, during which the children were told that they had been commissioned by the museum to investigate Tom Crean's life, especially his experiences on the *Terra Nova* expedition. Having examined the expedition, the children are now asked to consider which moments from Crean's life could be depicted in the museum, and to consider how best to depict these moments. They are firstly asked to sculpt key moments in Crean's life. (**Mantle of the expert**)

- Divide the children into pairs (A's and B's). Instruct one member of each pair to sculpt his partner into a shape which depicts Crean at this moment. Discuss implicit meanings. Ask children to consider an appropriate caption for each sculpture. Reverse the order.

- Instruct children to work in groups of four and to consider using a variety of media which could be employed to commemorate Crean. Encourage them to consider the following possibilities: poetry, song, music, dance, drama, mime or visual art. Provide children with a number of weeks to complete their projects.

- Following the sharing of each piece encourage the children to engage in a post-reflection discussion:
    - *Discuss style of expression.*
    - *Discuss the effectiveness of the group's approach.*
    - *Discuss the underlying meaning inherent in the piece.*
    - *Compare and contrast the different approaches which were used by the children.*

▶ Conclusion: Personal Engagement with Theme and Integration

- Draw a time line of different dreams that people, or the children themselves, may have at different stages in their lives. Explore how dreams and ambitions change, as one grows older.

- Explore the poem 'Hold Fast to Dreams' (Appendix 4).

Other information points

Tom Crean was awarded the Albert medal for bravery and courage and a naval good conduct medal.

Integration

EXAMPLES FROM *TOM CREAN* DRAMA	SUBJECT/STRAND	SKILLS
Improvisations • Scott and government official • Crean and his uncle • Scott and Crean • Crew depositing supplies • Crean, Lashly and Evans en route to base camp	**English (oral language)** Strand: Competence and confidence in using language; Developing cognitive abilities through language	• Using language to persuade argue, defend and express emotions.
Preparing advertisements	**English (writing)** Strand: Emotional and imaginative development through writing Art design and making	• Employing appropriate strategies to sell advertising. Media awareness. Designing a poster. • Naming similarities and differences
At the fair	**Geography** Strand: Connections between the past and the present	
	Maths	• Making a price list of cattle purchased and sold.
	SPHE	• Exploring values, ambitions and goals.

PART TWO: IMPROVISATION

What Is Improvisation?

Improvisation is used throughout this book as a way of generating meaning. In the chapter dealing with early childhood play, the notion that children spontaneously improvised with fictional roles in order to test, try out and play with ideas about the world was discussed. The *Winter's Dilemma* drama highlighted the way in which character and theme can be developed while the children and teacher improvise during a teacher-in-role encounter. In *The Children of Lir* drama, the children improvised through movement and music as they 'danced' a holistic response to the circumstances that the characters found themselves in. This section will focus particularly on the use of *verbal* improvisations in a process drama, which aim to provide a deeper insight into character and situation.

Verbal improvisation can be defined as the ability to make-up or explore in an unscripted 'as if' situation. It takes place when participants step into role and in so doing gain an insight into a character's perspective through the generation of spontaneous focused dialogue. The focused nature of the generated dialogues is due to thoughtful input from the teacher prior to the improvisation. While children improvise, attitudes and feelings pertaining to a character's situation are uncovered and unknown information about the character is developed.

The participant (child) operates in both the fictional and the real world and as a result fictional meanings can be connected with the child's own experience. As is the case with all artistic encounters, experiencing the art form also facilitates growth in artistic ability. Therefore, as children become more adept at improvisation, they will learn to use gesture, voice and movement to signify and depict character and situation. This results in children making meaning and becoming meaning-makers concurrently.

▶ *Historical Background*

The genesis of improvisation can be traced back to the origins of story. Storytelling was a very important part of the oral tradition during pre-writing times. It acted as a channel to transmit rituals, beliefs and values (wisdom) from one generation to the next. Stories also served as a way in which oral societies kept the history of their cultural group alive. Consequently, the storyteller was held in high regard and often had status equal to that of societal leaders.

These early stories provided the raw material for early-improvised theatre. Actors improvised in order to develop character, plot and extend the dialogue embedded in the stories. Over the centuries, many different improvisational styles have been adopted in various theatre contexts. The most direct ancestor of modern improvisation is probably the *Commedia dell'Arte*, which was popular throughout Europe beginning in the mid-1500s. Troupes of performers would travel from town to town, presenting improvised shows in public squares and on makeshift stages. Improvisation continues to be widely used by theatre practitioners today.

THE IMPROVISATION PROCESS

In the next section we will discuss the improvisation process in three stages: before improvisation, during improvisation and after improvisation.

Before Improvisation

Choosing moments

As some children may find verbal improvisations challenging, the teacher will need to consider a number of factors before children engage in an improvisation. The appropriate choice of moment will be central to the process. You will notice that all of the improvised moments in the *Tom Crean* drama were chosen so that new discoveries could be made about unknown events. For example, an improvisation was set up to explore the way that Tom reacted when Scott dismissed him. The new discoveries, which were made as a result of this improvisation, broadened the children's understanding of the character's situation and of the underlying themes of the drama. However, while we must be careful to choose moments that are open enough to facilitate new discoveries in drama, we must also be careful to provide sufficient teacher support to launch the improvisation. Lack of teacher support can result in children failing to engage in improvisations and to benefit educationally and artistically from the experience.

Children will need to receive some support in relation to stepping into the fictional time and place of a moment. Guided imagery and mime can be employed for this purpose. Once children have been given a chance to become familiar with the time and place of a moment, the teacher will need to consider the use of dramatic tension to enhance engagement and learning.

▶ *Dramatic Tension*

Dramatic tension is an essential component of any improvisation as it is the fuel which challenges the characters and motivates the children whilst in role. It adds energy to the explorative moment and acts as an engagement device for the participants. It challenges children to delve deeper into the characters' situations and to engage with the underlying themes of the drama. Structuring for dramatic tension requires some insight into the notion of character motivation. When a character enters an improvisation he will be guided by a certain perspective or attitude relating to the forthcoming circumstance. This attitude or perspective can be described as character motivation. Character motivation provides the impetus for each character to continue dialoguing.

In process drama, dramatic tension is experienced when a child-in-role discovers that his motivation is at odds with another role. Tension is created as each character tries to negotiate his personal motivations with the other character while reacting to the challenges the other character presents. This creates a dilemma for those involved. This occurred in the Crean workshop when Scott's intention to dismiss Crean was at odds with Crean's hopes of going to the South Pole. A conflict of interest also existed in the earlier stages of the drama between Crean's interest in travel and his uncle's desire that Crean should stay at home and support his father. As a result of such tensions, the children engaged directly with the themes of the drama.

Certain strategies can be employed by the teacher to reinforce or heighten the existing tension inherent in an improvisation. These strategies can also be used to create further challenges for the characters to resolve. In the Crean drama, additional tension was added by:

* Constraining the characters.
* Highlighting a character's existing anxiety.
* Withholding existing information from a character.
* Challenging a character.

The above approaches will now be illustrated using the improvisation which took place when Scott had the task of dismissing Crean from the expedition.

▶ *Scott Dismisses Crean*

Constraining Scott
Scott was prevented from rushing into dismissing Crean too quickly by being reminded of the exceptional relationship that had existed between the men in the past. This increased the dramatic tension of the forthcoming improvised moment and ensured that those 'in role' as Scott engaged with

---

the challenges and the complexities of the situation in a fruitful way. It also prevented the situation from turning into an unproductive conflict.

Reinforcing a character's emotional anxiety

Emphasising the bond which had developed between the two men also served to reinforce Scott's emotional anxiety and guilt about his forthcoming task. Reminding Scott of Crean's lifelong ambition to reach the Pole further highlighted the anxiety that Scott felt. Therefore, inserting this smaller tension further increased the character's dilemma, the character's anxiety and consequently the dramatic tension of the moment. A strong tension existed between Scott's desire to dismiss Crean versus his close relationship with Crean.

Crean's anxiety was in turn reinforced by asking the children-in-role as Crean to reflect on questions such as *How are you feeling? What do you expect the news to be? How will you react if the news is not in your favour?*

Withholding information

Consciously withholding the impending news from Crean that he would not be going to the Pole reinforced his vulnerability and created a suspense which would further increase the dramatic tension of the moment for the character. Withholding this information also created a mismatch between one character's expectations and the reality of what he was to discover about his future.

Challenging character

Asking those in role as Crean if he would be willing to sit back and accept his fate if the outcome was not in his favour, built on the tension of the moment and ensured that Scott's task would not be easy.

▶ Briefing

The way in which the teacher assists children in identifying their potential motivation for engaging in an improvisation is commonly known as 'briefing'. As the content of the section above suggests, the Tom Crean drama provided examples of a variety of ways in which briefing can take place before and during an improvisation to increase dramatic tension. In the next section, we will discuss these in terms of two principal approaches: general briefing and specific briefing

- **General briefing:** In this case, the content of the pre-improvisation discussion will be derived from the children's current understanding of the characters in question and the inherent tension of the situation. The teacher's task here is to help the children to articulate their current knowledge and understanding through her questioning. The teacher usually chooses general briefing over specific briefing when the inherent tension in a situation is strong enough to maintain interest and motivation, and when the children have already engaged in significant exploration of the characters in question.

- **Specific briefing:** In this case, the content of the brief is predominantly generated by the teacher through the insertion of increased tension. This tends to involve the teacher providing a clear indication to the children of the motivations for the roles in question. These motivations are often deliberately in conflict with each other, which provides the children with the challenge of negotiating in the context of differing perspectives. The teacher generally chooses specific briefing over general briefing when either the inherent tension of a situation is not strong enough to provide motivation for the characters in question, when the children have little knowledge of the characters to date, or when the teacher feels that children's general engagement with the drama could be stronger and needs more support.

In summary, the teacher's choice of approach to briefing will depend on a number of key factors namely:

- The stage of the drama in which the improvisation takes place.
- The level of tension already inherent in a situation.
- The children's knowledge of the roles/characters in question to date.
- The children's level of participation in the drama to date.

The following are examples of ways in which general and specific briefing approaches were used in the Tom Crean drama.

▶ *Example of General Briefing*

Improvisation: Crean, Lashly and Evans are asked to return to base camp (p. 106)
In advance of this improvisation, the children as crew members had physically and emotionally invested in the ambition of reaching the South Pole before being asked to return to base camp. They were, therefore, likely to understand the depth of disappointment which the men felt at the time of their dismissal. This knowledge helped the children to build on their chosen roles and to react to the tension of the situation. It also helped them to decide on their character's perspective, motivation and attitude to the situation.

In this case, reflective questions are used before the improvisation to enable the children to consider their current knowledge and understanding of the situation. Such questions will also deepen children's engagement and commitment to the improvisation e.g. *What was the mood like between the men as they faced the long journey back to base camp? How might this mood be conveyed? How might the characters make these feelings known?*

> ### ▶ Example of Specific Briefing

Improvisation: Crean and his uncle on the way home from the fair (p. 97)
Tension was increased during this improvisation by specifically reminding those in role as Crean about the way the storyteller influenced his desire to travel overseas. In addition, reminding Crean that he must do his best to let his dreams be known to his uncle, further strengthened this tension. The contrast between Crean's desire to travel and his uncle's desire for Crean to remain at home were reinforced by the teacher when she reminded Crean's uncle to do his best to entice Crean to consider the land.

▶ Summary

As you can see, differences exist in terms of when it is best to use either specific or general briefing. Specific briefing tends to be more direct than general briefing. Specific briefing is used when the children need extensive support in terms of building their understanding of the situation, and ensuring that an inherent tension exists between the characters. This kind of support is deemed necessary because the children have not gained experiential knowledge of the situation leading up to the improvisation. On the other hand, general briefing tends to be more indirect as children are left to decide their own character motivation and build on the tension of the moment without direct teacher support. It was emphasised that the experiential knowledge they gained about the situation being explored from earlier stages of the drama enabled them to do this.

Whatever the nature of support offered to the children, the outcome of the improvisation must remain open-ended. It should be entirely up to each child to find ways of negotiating in role. It must also be remembered that despite a character's motivation, or attitudes towards a certain situation at the outset, the unpredictable nature of any interaction between human beings means that a character may change his intended course of action or perspective during the improvisation. This may happen as he begins to see the other character's perspective of events. With this in mind, the teacher's intention should at no point involve prescriptively telling the children what to say or how to say it. This would inhibit the children from spontaneous involvement and would be in conflict with the underlying principle of improvisation.

During Improvisation

While the children are participating in improvisation the teacher's main objective is to ensure that children are authentically engaging with the experience.

Initially engaging in whole class scanning will provide the teacher with an opportunity to make some general observations about the children's ability to believe in the fiction. Following this the teacher can now begin to further investigate individual children's efforts by moving around the space and discretely listening to the children's discussions. The subtle nature of the teacher's observations means that she is acting as a bystander and an audience to the children's efforts. From this standpoint, she will be seeking to discover how well the children are able to negotiate in role and deal with the challenges that the other characters are presenting. The subtle nature of this stage also protects the children and gives them freedom to engage with the improvised situation without interruption.

▶ Reflective Questions

Once the teacher feels that the children have been given enough time to engage in the improvisation, it may be helpful to pause the discussion to give time for reflection. They might privately reflect on questions such as the following in role:

- *Are you happy with the way the conversation is progressing?*
- *What have you learned about the character so far?*
- *Is there anything else you need to say at this stage?*
- *Are you happy with your ability to take on the role?*

Through this reflective process the child will become more aware of the fact that making meaning is an active process and involves using and reading verbal and non-verbal signifiers to create and interpret meaning. Such reflection can also serve to increase dramatic tension in the situation. It can also help the children to come to an understanding of the way the fictional meaning can apply to the child's own life.

▶ Spotlighting (optional)

Once children have been given enough time to invest in the situation being explored, brief sections of the improvisation can be shared using a non-threatening technique called spotlighting. This involves spotlighting individual pairs while they are improvising and asking them to continue the improvisation unrehearsed. This shared moment should not go beyond thirty seconds. When children have shared their improvisations the teacher can ask the observers (children) to reflect on the content of what they have seen and heard.

After Improvisation

This stage of the improvisation process happens after children have concluded the improvisation. At this stage the children are provided with an opportunity to further amalgamate the knowledge and ideas they have encountered during the improvisation. This is best achieved by sharing the different meanings which were generated during the improvisation. There are numerous ways in which this can be achieved. Each approach will now be outlined.

▶ Sharing Meaning

Questioning

Children can be enabled to engage in reflection as individuals, or they can share their responses to the improvisation with their partner or group. We recommend that questions related to both content (theme related) and dramatic form be reflected upon.

Examples of reflective questions

- *What happened between the characters during the improvisation?*
- *Did any tension exist between the characters?*
- *Did this create any problems for the characters?*
- *What strategies did each character use to convey his feelings? Which strategy was particularly effective?*

The children's responses can then be shared with the entire class. Publicly sharing ideas in this way develops the learning potential of the improvisation as it gives the children an opportunity to hear different experiences. This reinforces the idea that a variety of meanings and interpretations can emerge from the same improvisation.

▶ *Isolating Text and Developing Subtext (Optional)*

Some children might be at the stage where they wish to share their improvisations. This activity involves enabling children to dissect and analyse the dialogue which emerged during the improvisation. To do this the children will firstly deconstruct the improvisation by reflecting on and choosing a significant piece of dialogue (approximately three sentences) which took place between the characters during the improvisation. Asking the children to choose dialogue which represents a moment of tension is a useful way of focusing them on their chosen piece of dialogue. Once the children are given an opportunity to rehearse the piece, they can then be asked to share its content with another pair or indeed with the rest of the class.

When the children have been given a chance to develop the dialogue, the subtext of the piece can then be examined. This can be achieved by asking another pair to observe the piece and to consider what the character might say if he was being truthful to himself at this time.

Footnotes

1   *An Unsung Hero* by Michael Smith.
2   Alternatively, the children could physicalise the fair by becoming musicians, magicians, sellers or storytellers; the teacher could go around to each group in role as Tom and observe the day's happenings.
3   Consult Section 2 of this chapter for the theory associated with the use of dramatic tension in process drama.

Chapter 6
USING SCRIPT AS A STIMULUS FOR DRAMA

(Fourth to Sixth Class)

Introduction

> *Children can be led to see script as an invitation to create action . . . action can be used as a pre-text for a fuller drama.*
>
> (*Drama Curriculum Teacher Guidelines*, 1999, p. 16)

This chapter explores ways in which script can be used as a pre-text for the creation and representation of dramatic action. Process drama will be used for this purpose. Exploring text in this way enables children to deconstruct, expand and create dramatic text of their own. As a result, children do not solely rely on the author's meaning. While children create their own meaning, they will simultaneously engage both cognitively and emotionally with the content of the script: the situation, the characters and the theme. In addition they will learn about the way the art form can be used to manipulate content and the way content can be used to manipulate form (Greene, 1995). An adapted script from the screenplay *Rabbit-Proof Fence* by Christine Olsen will be used to illustrate artistic and pedagogical points throughout this chapter.

This chapter also provides ideas in relation to the way meaning can be represented using scriptwriting and performance. In other words it examines ways of moving from process to performance and therefore it incorporates the full range of experiences within the subject (process-product). Performance is explored in this chapter through scripts which by their nature are written to be performed. This does not necessarily imply that all scripts should be performed to an outside audience. Performing to an outside audience should be seen as an optional course of action. In recent times the notion of performance has taken on a broader definition in that it also embraces sharing work with one's peers in the confines of the classroom.

▶ Traditional Approaches to Script

The notion of exploring script through process drama challenges the traditional way in which script was dealt with in schools. A very traditional approach to script could focus on children learning lines for a formal performance. Reproducing what is written on the page without interpreting and exploring the content and form of the piece diminishes the quality of the performance. It often happens that a child's outgoing nature is the criteria used by the teacher to select the principle characters. Those who are not deemed confident are often given subservient parts; they become the flowers, trees and so on. Such an approach to the school play can amount to a 'superficial playing out of event' and can be 'accompanied by a degree of showing off' (O'Neill and Lambert, 1982, p. 25). Explorative questions are often not addressed, such as why did the character behave in this way? Does this action depict the character's inner feelings? How might we convey the complexity of this character's inner feelings using gesture?

In the following section we will begin to examine approaches to script which seek to take the best from traditional approaches and address the problems which have been outlined above.

▶ Summary of Chapter Direction

- **Section 1: Interpreting scripts; improvisation**
- **Section 2: Scripting dramatic text; shaping dramatic ideas as a playwright**
- **Section 3: Representation and meaning; from process to performance**

Rabbit-Proof Fence: Play Text

Short scenes will be chosen from the screenplay *Rabbit-Proof Fence*. This is an example of a play text which can be used with children from fourth to sixth class. The scenes themselves will be outlined in the next section. All the explorative ideas can be followed in chronological order, or certain ideas can be explored in isolation. The scriptwriting and performance sections are optional stages. It is intended that the guidelines offered can be applied to other scripts.

A discussion on script would be incomplete without some reference to script selection. It is best to choose scripts which have an obvious dramatic tension and those which lend towards character development and thematic exploration. Choosing scripts which are more open-ended in terms of character and theme ensure that children can create additional dramatic narratives.

▶ Background Story

Rabbit-Proof Fence explores the lives of three Aboriginal children, Molly, Gracie and Daisy. In 1931 these children were taken from their home in Jigalong, Western Australia by government officials to a native settlement in Moore River. It was customary at that time to send Aboriginal children from mixed backgrounds away to be educated and trained, as it was believed that this would enhance the children's lives. Unfortunately, from the perspective of the Aboriginal people, this deed resulted in the separation of families from each other and the beginning of a breakdown in Aboriginal culture. Children that were taken from their homes in this way are referred to as the 'stolen generation'.

After some time in the Moore River settlement, Molly decided to escape with Daisy and Gracie back to their home. This was no easy journey, as Molly was now faced with leading the children 1,600 kilometres back to Jigalong. Part of the journey involved following the 1,000-mile rabbit-proof fence home. The children encountered many problems along the way. One significant incident took place when Gracie challenged Molly's decision about the direction of the route she was taking and as a result decided to go it alone. Unfortunately, this act resulted in her capture and consequent return to Moore River settlement. Molly and Daisy succeeded in reaching Jigalong. Molly eventually got married and had children. Sadly these children were subsequently taken away from her.

Many efforts have been made to change the policy of separating children from their parents. In 1927, the Aboriginal activist Maynard demanded that such children be left with their parents and that Aboriginal culture be respected and nurtured. Later, in the 1970s, the Aboriginal Childcare Agency was established in Victoria and South Australia to help children who had been removed from their homes. In the 1980s most state governments agreed that Aboriginal families should not be separated. A national reconciliation process has been commenced in Australia involving both Aboriginal and non-Aboriginal communities.

This script provides children with an opportunity to engage in dialogue with the story of the 'stolen generation'. It explores themes such as identity and determination. Integrating this lesson with geography and history would undoubtedly give children a deeper understanding of the rich culture of these people.

A selection of five adapted scenes will now be presented from the *Rabbit-Proof Fence* screenplay. Adaptations have been made to the order of each scene, and to the dialect in an effort to make the text more accessible for children. The narrative introduction to some scenes has also been altered or cut, as it was felt that some of the information provided may not have made sense for the children as it is presented out of context.

The scene order has also been changed e.g. the capture scene originally appeared as an earlier scene in the screenplay. This has now been placed as a flashback scene when Molly is in Moore River. This move was made due to the high emotional intensity of the scene. It is hoped that postponing the scene will ensure that children will have built up enough emotional investment in the context prior to its exploration, and that it will prevent children from responding in a superficial way to the moment of capture. The children's life in Moore River will firstly be explored, followed by the capture and finally the scene outlining the children's return journey along the rabbit-proof fence.

❱ *Rabbit-Proof Fence*

Scene 1

The dining hall:	Moore River
Purpose:	Children are initiated into life at Moore River (context building)
Who:	Molly, Gracie, Daisy and George (staff member)
Where:	Breakfast at the dining hall
When:	A few days after arrival

The morning after the children arrive, everybody is wearing the same outfit. The girls have not received their uniforms yet. Children queue and receive porridge. Molly takes a plate of grey sludge and goes to sit on a bench, Gracie and Daisy join her. Molly watches as all the children stuff the porridge into their mouths and gulp down tea. Daisy pushes the plate away and murmurs to Molly in her own language.

Daisy:	Rubbish food. (Spoken in native tongue)
George:	You have to talk English here, now eat.

Daisy, tears welling, picks out a tiny piece of porridge, puts it in her mouth, shudders and retches. Molly pushes a tin of tea to her. Daisy, blinded by tears, gulps, swallows. Gracie, big eyed, watches it all. George moves on. Molly deftly swaps plates with Daisy and begins to eat.

Scene 2
The sewing room, morning

Purpose: To explore efforts made to help the children settle into Moore River
Who: Molly, Gracie, Daisy, Miss Jessop, Matron, Nina
Where: The sewing room
When: A few days after arrival

Miss Jessop is kneeling putting an old shirt over Daisy's head. Gracie whispers to Molly (in native language).

Gracie: New clothes.

Miss Jessop glances over to them.

Miss Jessop: You have to speak English here.
She throws two shirts and two pairs of shoes from the shelf down to Molly and Gracie.
Put these on.

Matron enters

Matron: They look like Moore River girls now, don't they, Miss Jessop?
Nina: Take them to the nursery, show them how to sweep.

Scene 3
The capture

Purpose: To examine the challenge faced by Molly, Gracie and Daisy and their mothers on the day of the capture
Who: Molly, Gracie, Daisy, Constable Riggs, Maude (Molly's mother), Lilly (Gracie's mother), Hungerford
Where: At their home in Jigalong
When: The moment before the children were captured by Riggs

The weekly rations are being prepared for distribution to the Aboriginal people by Hungerford. He counts each item: blankets, flour, sugar, tobacco, tins of bully beef. The girls' mother, the girls and others saunter over to the depot. The group is relaxed and laughing . . . they return after receiving their goods.

It is Molly who hears the car first. She screws up her eyes against the glare. In the distance Gracie and Daisy look up. Maude and Lilly turn . . . they all stand and watch, curious as the car makes its way towards them.

→

The sun reflects off the windscreen, masking the driver. The car pulls to a stop. They watch as the door opens and Constable Riggs steps out wearing his uniform: blue jacket, silver buttons, moleskin trousers, and boots. Maude and Lilly see the policeman and know instantly why he has come. They cry out loud and urgently to the children, clutching their bags to them. The children are still playing . . . they look up at the women, Molly signs to them to come, and then she too runs after the women. The girls follow.

Riggs examines the behaviour. He gets back in the car, revs the engine and speeds after them. The car easily overtakes the group. Riggs circles around and pulls up a little towards them. The women are trapped by the fence. They look frantically towards the camp calling out shrilly. The door opens. Riggs steps out holding his papers.

Riggs:	Maude, I've come for the girls – orders from Mr Neville, they're to go to school.
	(The girls are removed. Daisy is taken first, followed by Gracie. Maude has hold of Molly.)
	I have the papers Maude; it's the law. There's nothing you can do, old lady.
Maude:	That's my child. I have reared her.
Riggs:	Mr Neville is their legal guardian.
Maude:	Those girls are our own children, they were brought up here.
Riggs:	It's the law Maude, you have no say. *(He drags Molly away.)*

Scene 4
Escaping Moore River

Purpose:	To explore the moment the children departed Moore River
Who:	Molly, Gracie and Daisy
Where:	The dormitory
When:	Minutes before the children escape

Molly decided the night before that she and her two sisters were not staying in Moore River. As the other girls left the dormitory for school, Molly called her two sisters to her.

Gracie:	Where we going?
Molly:	We are going home to mother.
Daisy:	How are we going to get home?
Molly:	Walk.
Gracie:	We are not going, are we Molly?
Molly:	It's going to rain. We got to go now.
Daisy:	Can we take our dresses?
Gracie:	It's too far, Molly.
Molly:	Come, Gracie. Now . . . get your shoes.

Scene 5
Returning home

Purpose: To examine the intensity of the journey home as a disagreement emerges between Molly and Daisy

Who: Molly, Gracie and Daisy

Where: Along the rabbit-proof fence

When: A few days after the escape

A gravel road cuts across the fence. Molly and Gracie argue while Daisy sits watching a line of caterpillars.

Gracie: We can get to Wiluna, catch the train.

Molly: They'll catch us Gracie. The worst bit is finished, all finished, this is the best way.

Gracie: Jigalong is too far, Molly. We can get to Wiluna easy.

Molly: It's easy alright, easy for them to find us. Catch us.

Gracie: But Molly, my mummy is at Wiluna. She is there.

Gracie sets off away from them, down the road, head down, determined. Daisy comes to stand next to Molly and grabs a piece of Molly's skirt with one hand, big eyes watching. Gracie turns, stands there, defiant.

Molly: Don't go on the road, Gracie, not on the road. Come with us around for a bit and then go in. Come with us this way.

Gracie begins to walk on the road away from them. The following morning Molly decides to look for Gracie. They find Gracie huddled in the railway track. As they watch a car approaches and Sergeant Mills gets out and after a struggle captures Gracie.

Molly and Daisy continue and eventually reach home. When they arrive, Molly runs towards (her mother) Maude's arms; she is held by her mother.

Molly's final narrative

We walked for nine weeks, a long way from home. I got married, and I had two baby girls. Then they took me and my kids back to that place, Moore River. And I walked all the way back to Jigalong again carrying Annabella. When she was three that Mr Neville took her away. I never saw her again. Gracie is dead now. She never made it back to Jigalong. Daisy and me, we're here living in our country, Jigalong.

Section 1: Interpreting Scripts; Improvisation

Viewing drama as a living art form means that responding to text needs to be done practically. To do this, verbal improvisation can be combined with image making and movement when exploring character and situation. This process enables the child to connect verbal and non-verbal elements of drama – the voice and the body. Interpreting text using the body and the voice also enables children to engage with its complexities and inherent themes. Dewey advocates the importance of the body as a means of accessing knowledge, claiming that what is performed by the body and experienced through the senses is more accessible than other kinds of learning. Therefore, exploring text in this way is far superior to over-emphasising an intellectual response.

The first stage of script exploration should involve children reading each scene so that they can generate some initial responses. Following this, children should be led to create their own dramatic moments by exploring the characters interacting in other contexts e.g. additional moments before the capture, happy moments in Moore River, or life after the children escaped, could be developed. Practical ways of interpreting script will now be discussed under the following headings. All of the ideas are presented as options, which the teacher may choose to use or adapt.

- Initial response to script using discussion
- Context-building activities
- Character development
- Scene development

▶ *Interpreting Script: Discussion*

The importance of not over-emphasising an intellectual response when it comes to the exploration of script has already been highlighted. At this stage, interpreting script using discussion should only serve to provide information about the chronological order of the story and initial character information. The information gathered in this way is important before any deeper exploration can take place.

Enabling children to firstly research the historical background against which this story is set is also important, as it will be difficult to proceed without this knowledge. The internet, documentaries and newspaper articles can be consulted in this regard. Once this research has been conducted, distribute the script to the children and explore the following questions.

Background story
- What information does this scene provide?
- Whose story is being told?
- Why is this story being told (theme question)?
- What background events led to the removal of the children from their homeland (political question)?
- Create a storyboard of the main events and the actions of the characters in each scene.

Chapter 6 USING SCRIPT AS A STIMULUS FOR DRAMA

Character reflection
- Who are the central characters in each scene? Where are they? What is going on?
- Identify a significant line of dialogue which emphasises each character's desires during the moment depicted in the scene.

General question

In pairs, list words which describe the mood of each scene. Support the answer with some evidence from the script.

▶ *Interpreting Script: Building Context*

A game-like approach will be used to explore the context of the script. Using games at this early stage is a useful way of initiating children into practical work. Simultaneously children will gain a deeper understanding of the different places the characters inhabited e.g. Jigalong, Moore River and the rabbit-proof fence. The nature of this exploration is an important prelude before character exploration. Examples of context-building activities will now be provided.

▶ *Options*

Pastimes in Jigalong

Organise children in to a circle

- Ask the entire class to think of something the girls did in Jigalong. The children are told that this mime/action needs to be linked in some way with the natural environment. Explain that it could be a pastime or a job associated with the place e.g. hunting. Continue the game by asking one child to share this action with the class; the next child has to identify the action and mime a new action etc.

- Divide the children into groups of three and advise them to decide on a game that the three girls might have played in Jigalong. Once the children have been given ample time to discuss and play the game, ask them to teach or play their game with another group.

Exploring Moore River

- Ask the children to break into groups of four in order to become one of the girls or the matron. Explain that the children were warmly greeted by the matron when they arrived at Moore River. Explain that the children-in-role as matron will show the children around the settlement. The children are told that matron made every effort to impress the children as she wanted to give a positive impression of the settlement.

Follow the leader (leaving Moore River)
- Divide the children into groups of three. Ask them to imagine that they are Molly, Gracie or Daisy. After the escape tell the children that they are going to play a game of follow the leader.

- Explain that as this was a treacherous journey, Molly will have to do her best to guide the children safely across the terrain. Encourage the child-in-role as Molly to verbalise what the others have to do along the way e.g. *we are going to crawl out of the settlement . . . now we are going to cross this river, be careful of the crocodiles, they look very hungry today . . .*
(Background music can be used to create atmosphere.)

Map-making
- Draw a map of the area named Jigalong, identify all the important places the children and their parents frequented.

- Draw a map outlining the places the children might have passed en route from Jigalong to Moore River (consult an atlas).

Guided imagery
- The children are asked to close their eyes and to imagine they are Molly thinking back over what happened when she returned. As she does she visualises her life in Jigalong and the journey she made along the rabbit-proof fence.

Rabbit-proof fence
- What does the fence look like?
- What colour is it?
- What does it feel like to touch?
- Is it easy or difficult to walk across the terrain?
- Relive the challenges and the happy moments you encountered.

▶ *Interpreting Script: Character Development*

Once children have been given an opportunity to establish the 'who', 'where', 'what' and 'when' of each scene, and once they have begun to broaden their understanding of the context, time can now be devoted to developing children's deeper understanding of character. This is an important process as it is not possible to immediately step into a role without sufficient prior exploration. Character exploration involves examining the private world of a character: his interests, pastimes and his attitudes about a particular issue or situation. It also involves gaining insight into a character's thoughts which he may not openly disclose.

Hot seating or thought tracking is a useful way of tapping into a character's inner thoughts. For example, when Riggs (teacher–in–role) was hot seated by children in a school setting, it was revealed that a tension existed between Riggs's duty to his profession and his view of the deeds he had to conduct on a daily basis. It became apparent that he was very perturbed about having to remove the children from their homeland, but nevertheless felt that he had no choice. In the school setting improvisation was then used to create new dramatic action arising out of the information which was established through the hot seat. The interaction which could have taken place between Riggs and his wife the evening after he removed the children was improvised. This dramatic moment revealed new stories about the character and the situation.

The following outlines process drama approaches, which can be used to develop character.

Paper placement
Encourage children to work in pairs and to cut out paper symbols which represent the furniture and belongings of a character's personal space e.g. Molly's bedroom at home, her bedroom at Moore River. Encourage children to physically place the furniture or personal belongings in the space. Deciding what objects a character might possess and locating these in the space will deepen children's understanding of character. Major or minor characters can be explored in this way.

Using objects/props
Playing with objects is a useful way of developing character and situation. Ask children to think about what objects the children in the story might have valued for personal reasons before the capture. A scene could be improvised which emphasised the importance of these objects. Alternatively, ask the children to think about and to improvise around the events associated with a significant object.

Hot seating

As was already highlighted hot seating is a useful way of getting children to gain a deeper knowledge of a character's inner beliefs and attitudes. It also enables children to gain an understanding of how characters perceive their relationships with other characters. The teacher generally assumes the hot seat, as she is in a better position to create tension and broaden the character's biography.

Example of characters that could be hot seated:

- Riggs before he has to capture the children and after he captured the children
- When Molly first arrives at Moore River
- Gracie after she leaves Molly and Gracie
- The matron of Moore River

Developing a character's profile

(Adapted from Hodgson and Richards, 1966)

Establish general information about a character by dividing the children into groups of three or four to work on the following questions:

- General description based on evidence from the text
- Age
- Favourite pastime
- Most significant moment in their lives
- Most challenging moment in their lives to date
- What does the character do when he is alone?
- What do others say about him?

Role on the wall

Role on the wall involves representing a character in pictorial form. The character's outline is drawn on a page and students are asked to consider words which they would use to describe the character. Doing this before or after a hot-seat session can be very useful as it enables children to compare and contrast the character's attitudes before and after they meet the character.

Option A

- Personal view of self is listed inside the character's body outline.
- General perceptions that other characters have of him could be represented outside the outline e.g. community, family or friends.

➡

Option B
- What is known about the character is written inside the outline.
- What is unknown is written outside the outline.

Additional information, which is gleaned about the character as the workshop progresses, can be added to the role on the wall. Alternatively, children may want to remove misconstrued perceptions which were made about the character from the role on the wall.

Further written activities
- Compose a day in the life of a character e.g. the day Riggs captured the children.
- Use visual images to present a map of a character's life.

▶ Interpreting Script: Scene Development

Non-verbal improvisation: still image
(See Chapter 5 for further debate on using still image)

The removal from Jigalong
- Create a still image of an ordinary moment in the family or community's life before the children were captured. Use this moment to demonstrate in some way the close bond that existed between the children, their family and the community.

- Contrast this image by depicting an image of life in Jigalong three weeks later (difficult experience).

- Create a still image demonstrating the family trying to move on with their lives a year after the children have been removed. Thought tracking can be used to explore the inner thoughts of the characters.

Moore River settlement
- Create an image depicting the children settling in to the life at Moore River. What are they doing? Who are they with? What is it about this activity which makes them happy?

- Contrast this scene with the moment the children were confronted by George.

- Create a still image of the moment after George confronts Daisy in the canteen. Who was present? How did the outsiders react? Use thought tracking to explore the bystanders' reaction. Encourage children to use eye contact, and distance between characters to emphasise their reaction to what happened.

→

Journey along the rabbit-proof fence
- Create two images depicting the different ways the children might have got some food on their return home; one image can represent a positive experience and the other can represent a challenging moment.

- Create a sequence of still images depicting the slow divide which took place between Molly and Gracie.

Back in Jigalong
- Create an image of the reunion (represent this in slow motion, perhaps three consecutive images placed together).

- Create a moment depicting something Molly, Daisy and the family were doing a few weeks after their return to Jigalong.

Verbal improvisations: developing dialogue

Note: Dialogue can be added to each of the still images created earlier. Limit children to approximately three sentences or under per character.

Additional dramatic moments and dialogue can be developed through the following improvisations.

Moore settlement
- Improvise the reaction of two canteen workers who witnessed the incident between George and the girls. Tension can be inserted by privately briefing each worker in the following ways:
    - **Worker one:** She does not have any compassion for the children. She is not an Aboriginal worker.
    - **Worker two:** Disagrees with what happened, as she was once in this situation herself. As she is a private person she does not want to refer to her past during the exchange with the other worker.

- Create the conversation which took place between the matron and Miss Jessop when the children left the nursery.

- Improvise the moment Molly informed the girls that she intended to leave the settlement. Enable those in role as Molly to consider ways she will subtly prepare the children for departure given that the children have started to settle into Moore River.

After Moore River settlement
- Devise a scene depicting the interaction which took place between Daisy and Molly after Gracie went her separate way.

This section outlined ways in which the children could be helped to interpret the *Rabbit-Proof Fence* script. The next section outlines ways of approaching scriptwriting with children.

Improvisation: life in Jigalong

Scripting a scene

Section 2: Scripting Dramatic Texts

▶ *Scripting Dialogue*

Scripting scenes gives children an opportunity to become playwrights; it challenges them to use the knowledge they have gained about what constitutes a dramatic encounter to create and represent dialogue in a written manner. The previous section, which involved exploring the physical discourse of the text, expanded children's knowledge of existing scenes and helped them create new scenes. In effect, these new ideas can provide the raw material for the children to become scriptwriters. They can also assist children with performance work. With this in mind, the step from improvising to scriptwriting and indeed to performance should not present too much of a challenge for children. For example, they could script a scene before the capture; a scene demonstrating a positive experience and a not so positive experience the girls may have had at Moore River; or a scene depicting life after the girls returned. Further details on developing a performance will be outlined in the next section.

While children are engaged in the writing of a script, time should be given to discussing issues such as sentence length, punctuation and use of pause to enrich each scene. In addition, if children wish to develop a full script, their attention should also be drawn to the importance of developing context, character and dramatic tension. If children have experienced the Tom Crean drama their awareness can be drawn to the effects of dramatic tension in this drama.

If desired, the created script can be shared in an informal setting or it can become part of the raw material for a performance work. It is advisable that before children commence any scripted writing, a range of scripts, including the scenes in this chapter, should be made available to children so that they can investigate the different approaches used by the playwright.

▶ *Writing Original Plays*

As children get more comfortable with this way of working they could be asked to construct their own original script. Again they can be encouraged to contemplate context, characters and central tensions. The following ideas might prove helpful as a way of supporting children.

- Describe the main characters and the places which these characters will frequent. Will the action take place in the past, present or future?
- How will you develop the context?
- What role will minor characters have in the story?
- What challenging situations will the characters find themselves in? Does a tension exist between different characters' motivations?
- Will the characters change or develop as the story progresses?
- Will you include stage directions?

Section 3: Representation and Meaning; from Process to Performance

The earlier sections of this chapter examined different ways meaning can be represented using improvisation and scriptwriting. This section explores particular ways in which meaning can be represented using performance. The ideas suggested in this section will hopefully address some of the problems which were identified earlier in relation to performance work.

As performance work involves the interplay between actor (child performer) and audience, the children's task, with the help of the teacher, is to find ways of presenting their created interpretations to an audience. Audience can be interpreted in a formal way (parents) or in an informal way (sharing with one's peers). With this in mind the ideas presented in this section can be adopted if teachers wish to share moments internally (in the classroom) or to an outside audience.

The skills involved in sharing meaning in a formal or an informal setting are not dissimilar, both involve creating meaning using verbal, non-verbal and visual signifiers. Formal performance differs from 'sharing' in the sense that formal performance requires a rigorous rehearsal period before reaching the performance platform. The rehearsal period will give the children an opportunity to practise the more subtle aspects of imparting meaning to a audience e.g. pausing, pacing, focus, use of gesture, facial expression, eye contact, movement and tone of presentation. Children will have gained previous experience of employing these signifiers in each of the dramas outlined in this book. With this in mind, ways in which each of these elements can be 'polished' during the rehearsal process will be outlined in the next section. In addition, when it comes to formal performance, some consideration will need to be given to the more technical aspects of the performance (the *mise en scene*). This refers to the staging or the visual arrangement of a production e.g. use of setting, scenery, costumes, use of lighting, props, the movement of the actors and any other visual elements (Neelands and Dobson, 2000).

Reviewing each explorative moment, which has already been created using process drama (Sections 1 and 2) and identifying key scenes which could be represented, is a useful starting point. Once potential scenes have been chosen consideration can be given to playing with the linear order of scenes e.g. beginning at the end, or juxtaposing contrasting moments. For example, the moment Riggs tells Maude and Lilly that the children will be well cared for at Moore River could be juxtaposed with the moment the girls meet George in the canteen. Monologue can also be effectively employed as a way of giving the audience detail about the inner turmoil a character might be feeling e.g. Riggs after the capture.

◗ The Rehearsal Process

As has already been mentioned, the rehearsal process involves refining children's existing skill and knowledge in the use of the art form to create and communicate the internal meaning of a scene. The following describes some activities which will help children during the rehearsal period. New scenes, which have been created, or actual scenes from the screenplay can be used in conjunction with each activity. The first section deals with refining skills in relation to voice and movement. Developing skills in this area is deemed particularly important as 'tone of voice, volume, pace and pitch can be used to add or destroy the meaning or atmosphere of a script' (Kempe and Lockwood, 2000, p. 12).

Note: Some of the following ideas have been adapted from Kempe and Lockwood. All the ideas presented can be applied to any scene.

Voice
In pairs practise speaking the lines of the text in the following ways:

- Whisper lines
- Shout lines
- Vary volume and pitch
- Express lines e.g. using an indifferent, reassuring, nervous, unsure or hopeful tone
- Experiment with pace: fast, slow or changeable. What is the effect of slowing down or speeding up the pace?
- Repeat until children are happy that the vocal manner represents the group's intentions

---

Mime and gesture
- Having chosen a moment for representation e.g. moment of capture. Miming could be employed as a way of developing background activities a character might have engaged in before the capture. Ask children to mime an action that depicts what one of the girls might have been doing before the capture. Instruct the children to experiment and improvise with these actions. If performance is intended these actions could become the character's stage business.

→

Skill development

- Request children to first practise making the action larger and then smaller than what it is. Repeat the process, but this time take cognisance of the different levels the body can adopt while practising these actions (high or low). Additionally, play with slowing down or speeding up the action.

- Join up with another partner and play with the action. One child can imitate the movement of the other person.

- Ask the children to improvise ways of developing a reaction to Riggs as they go about their task. Encourage children to use eye contact, pausing and so on to achieve the desired effects.

Abstract demonstration of feelings

Ask children to identify and demonstrate one key emotion felt during a particular scene e.g. complete frustration felt by the mothers when the children were captured by Riggs. Encourage the children to use their bodies to demonstrate this emotion.

- If performance is being used consider ways this image might be included in a performance piece.

Using movement and space to explore character relationships

- Experimenting with space to show a close or a remote relationship between characters is a useful way of depicting subtleties which might exist between characters in a moment. This can be achieved by directing children to repeat a scene standing far apart and/or very close to each other (Kempe and Lockwood, 2000).

- The issue of power can be played with in a similar manner by examining what happens when a character turns his back, kneels down, speaks his lines standing on an object, turns his back and glances over his shoulder. Enable children to consider other ways power might be represented in the scenes between the following characters:
  - Maude and Riggs
  - The girls and George in the dining room
  - Miss Jessop and the children (sewing room)
  - When Gracie challenges Molly en route to Jigalong

Before a scene is ready for performance, the children should be asked to share their scene with the rest of the class or 'critical' observers. Framing the children as directors or theatre critics will provide them with additional motivation for this task. It is important that children are reminded to begin by focusing on the overall strengths of the scene. Following this the children should be encouraged to give constructive feedback. Direct children to comment on the following:

- How was the 'who', 'where' and 'what' of each moment conveyed? Would you make any recommendations?
- Is there any aspect of the scene which needs to be made clearer?
- What tension exists in the scene?
- Comment on the way the group is using space to depict character and situation.
- Are they employing mime, movement and gesture effectively?
- Are the group subtly depicting subtext?
- What changes would you recommend?

Rehearsing the moment the girls returned home

▶ *Conclusion*

Throughout this chapter dramatic literacy was developed as children were led to become more adept at interpreting and representing the meaning of a dramatic text. The earlier improvisation work enabled children to explore the content and structure of the script. Children later became familiar with the craft of play-writing by scripting moments which had been created. This provided children with an additional way of reflecting on the meaning inherent in the piece. The latter stage involved combining content and form to create and shape meaning for an internal or an external audience. When it comes to formal presentations, it was emphasised that children will need direction in relation to creating a polished production. It was also emphasised that formal performance should be seen as an optional course of action.

It is hoped that the guidelines given in this chapter will provide teachers and children with an understanding that a script should not be interpreted as having a fixed meaning, but instead script should be seen as a pre-text for children to make personal discoveries. A direct relationship exists between the early explorative stage and the quality of children's scriptwriting and performance work. The meaning which emanates from the earlier improvisations essentially acts as the raw material for the play-writing and performance stages.

Acknowledgment

Extract from *Rabbit-Proof Fence: the Screenplay* by Christine Olsen, © Christine Olsen 2002. Reproduced by permission from Currency Press Pty Ltd, Sydney, Australia.

Chapter 7
PROCESS DRAMA AND THEATRE

Introduction

This chapter highlights the wide variety of theatre experiences which should be part of a child's experience in the primary school and which can strongly contribute to a child's ability to engage with process drama. These experiences include child's play, process drama, theatre in education, children's theatre productions and children performing their own work. This spectrum is referred to as the drama continuum and will now be explained using examples from the Irish context where possible. The relationship between these areas, and in particular how they contribute to a child's engagement with process drama, will be outlined. As theatre is the common thread which connects each of these areas, a discussion will firstly take place outlining the ways in which the theatre art form is present in and has contributed to the distinct form of process drama.

Process Drama and Theatre

Until the recent past, certain tensions existed between the notions of drama and theatre in debates about the teaching of drama in schools. Some practitioners emphasised a theatre skills approach. Other practitioners perceived this practice to be associated with the development of technical skills. They rejected what they felt was an over emphasis on a 'theatre skills' approach and believed that prominence should be given to content exploration (drama in education). The practice which is illuminated in this book is termed process drama. Process drama relates to both theatre and education. It engages a child in a fictional situation which has some thematic relevance to the child's life.

Process drama has its roots in theatre and in fact is a genre of theatre. Neelands (2000, p. 107) claims that process drama is a 'delicate shift into theatre'. Both process drama and theatre involve taking on and interacting in role, in another place and time. An underlying tension such as a dilemma or a threat motivates the actions of those in role. Indeed, these elements connect with all aspects of the drama continuum.

Process drama also relies on the use of certain theatrical signs in order to engage children both artistically and educationally. Theatre sign systems such as gesture, words, objects, movement and music are manipulated by the body to create and represent meaning. Like actors in the rehearsal process, children are required to manipulate these theatre signs in an effort to make sense of particular situations which characters encounter. They have to 'think in and through the materials of the medium in which they are working and to manipulate and transform the materials' (O'Neill, 1995, p. 1). Drama conventions such as still image, movement, dance and verbal improvisation provide the means through which these theatre 'signs' are manipulated. There are also occasions in process drama when the teacher needs to manipulate sign to convey meaning. This especially happens when the teacher employs gesture, voice, and objects during a teacher–in–role encounter e.g. the teacher-in-role as Winter manipulated sign in order to convey to the children how Winter was being treated and to ask the children's help in making things better (*Winter's Dilemma* drama).

Like theatre, audience is an inherent part of process drama and according to O'Neill (1995, p. 118) completes the 'theatrical equation'. Participants in process drama operate as participants and audience at the same time. There are two distinct ways in which audience can be defined in process drama. While children engage in process drama they simultaneously become spectators to their own actions and as a result engage in self-reflection. In addition, during process drama children can also become an audience to their peers' actions. They do this by decoding the way sign was manipulated by the group to represent meaning e.g. children were asked to read the images of a situation in which Aoife decided that something had to be done about the children in *The Children of Lir* drama. Dialoguing about the inherent meaning either individually or with one's peers heightens children's understanding of the way sign can be used to create meaning.

It is important to note at this juncture that while theatrical elements may be present within process drama, the move towards a traditional notion of product (performance) is a development towards a distinct form of theatre. If such a development is chosen we recommend that performance should evolve out of process drama approaches similar to those used in this book. Beginning with process ensures that the artistic and educational values of the experience are given due attention. The progressive steps involved in moving children from process to performance were highlighted in the chapters dealing with the *Rabbit-Proof Fence* and *The Children of Lir* dramas. Indeed, performance theatre companies would also use these approaches during their rehearsal process. In summary, beginning with process enhances the quality of children's engagement with the final product.

Variety of Theatre Forms that Influence a Child's Experience

As suggested in the introduction to this chapter, while we emphasise the use of process drama in the classroom, we recommend that the child should have an experience of all theatre forms. In our experience the quality of a child's experience in relation to one art form is improved by their experience of the full drama continuum. As a child watches a play he will subconsciously gain a familiarity with the way theatrical conventions combine with content to create meaning. A variety of theatre companies are available throughout Ireland which greatly benefit children's experience of theatre and act as a useful educational support. The following section will outline these practices.

▶ *Theatre in Education*

Theatre in education (TiE) describes professional theatre companies which bring theatre to primary and secondary schools. The children's own school environment houses the theatre event. Team Educational Theatre Company and Graffiti Theatre Company are examples of TiE companies.

TiE companies offer schools a specific type of programme designed to merge artistic and educational objectives in an effort to meet the needs of young audiences. Children can operate as spectators and participants concurrently during the production. They can be asked to engage in the decision-making process about a character's course of action or about a pertinent issue embedded in the piece. A follow up workshop is also provided which seeks to explore the inherent themes within the play. In addition, teachers receive follow-up support from resource packs.

Children's theatre
Children's theatre groups engage in performing professional plays for children. These plays can be performed in a theatre space or in a school. Babaro (Galway), Barnstorm (Kilkenny), Cahoots (NI) and Red Kettle (Waterford) are among some of the children's theatre companies in existence in Ireland.

Outreach education

An outreach facility in a theatre enables children and teenagers to interact with plays and drama as participants and audience members. There are a variety of theatre houses throughout Ireland which provide excellent outreach programmes for children. The Abbey, Draíocht (Blanchardstown) and AXIS (Ballymun) are among some of the companies working in this way.

Youth theatre

Youth theatre work involves young people in the preparation and performance of group-devised or scripted plays. Dublin Youth Theatre and Waterford Youth Drama are among some of the youth theatre groups in Ireland.

The Ark (Eustace St., Dublin)

The Ark is a custom-built cultural centre which devotes itself exclusively to innovative arts programmes for, by, with and about children. The intimate nature of the theatre ensures that any visit will leave the child with an artistic experience which is both meaningful and engaging. Most of the programmes are produced in-house and are written by professional children's writers. The centre also welcomes visiting theatre companies.

▶ *National Drama Associations*

Association for Drama Education in Ireland (ADEI)

The association for Drama Education in Ireland aims to provide a forum where those who are interested in using drama in various educational settings in Ireland can provide support for each other. Workshops and conferences are held regularly.

The National Association for Youth Drama (NAYD)

The National Association for Youth Drama is an umbrella body for the development of youth theatre throughout the Republic of Ireland. It provides a service to children which enables them to partake in the devising and/or acting of plays.

Irish Institute of Drama and Communication (IDAC)

The Irish Institute of Drama and Communication provides speech and drama practitioners with support. Workshops are organised throughout Ireland for its members.

▶ *Conclusion*

This chapter emphasised that dramatic activity should be viewed as a continuum beginning with the early play of young children, incorporating process drama, theatre in education, children's theatre and children performing their own plays. A new era is now beginning in Ireland since the introduction of drama as a curriculum subject. It is hoped that this book will provide drama practitioners with an understanding of the philosophy and principles underpinning the subject. The importance of recognising both the unique nature of the art form and the underlying educational benefits was brought to the fore. With this in mind, it set out to illuminate the way in which theatrical conventions and elements can be shaped in process drama to achieve artistic and educational goals.

APPENDICES

Appendix 1

▶ Chapter 4 – The Children of Lir

The spell – Heaney M., *The Names upon the Harp*, Faber & Faber, London, 2000, p. 21

> '*Children of Lir, your good fortune is over. From now on waterfowl will be your family, and your cries will be mingled with the cries of birds.*'

(Continued below)

p. 22

> '*You will not be swans forever . . . but you will keep the shape of swans for nine hundred years. You will spend three hundred years here on Lake Derravaragh, three hundred on the Sea of Moyle, and the last three hundred years by the Atlantic Ocean. When a king from the North marries a queen from the South and you hear the sound of a bell pealing out a new faith, you will know that your exile is over. Till then, though you will have the appearance of swans you will keep your own minds, and your own hearts and your own voices, and your music will be so sweet that it will console all who hear it. But go away from me now for the very sight of you torments me.*'

Appendix 2

▶ Chapter 5 – The Adventures of Tom Crean

Description of Antarctica

Infrastructure
- Antarctica is the fifth largest continent in the world
- Half the size of Australia – five million square miles
- It represents 10 per cent of the world's land mass
- Most turbulent seas in the world
- Ice and snow cover 98 per cent of the continent
- Coldest (–90 Degrees Celsius), windiest (range between 80–200 miles an hour), driest and least populated continent on earth
- Most remote place on the planet: 1,000 km to Cape Horn, 2,400 km to New Zealand, 4,000 km to South Africa

Natural habitat
- Ice sheets: Great Ice Barrier largest floating ice sheet in the world (area as large as France)
- Glaciers – Beadmore Glacier – 100 miles long
- Encourage research on Antarctic animal life

Appendix 3

▶ *Scott's Curriculum Vitae*

- Joined royal navy – serving on ships from 1881–1887
- 1887–1888 attended Royal Navy College
- Achieved the highest marks in his class
- Served as an officer in the Mediterranean and at home

Previous expedition to the South Pole
- Scott learned from his mistakes, he realised that more preparation and training were required.
- He demonstrated good leadership skills as he effectively managed the crew. Many scientific discoveries were made during this expedition.
- He also set the most southerly record by coming within 410 miles of the South Pole.

Why he believes England should venture to the South Pole again
- They could gain knowledge and claim new land for England
- Antarctica is the last unexplored and most remote continent on earth
- There could be hidden reserves of oil and other mineral resources
- There is a sense of urgency as Norwegians also interested
- Advances can be made in science – marine biologists, glaciologists, geologists and meteorologists

Type of crew he is seeking
- Expert crew – scientists (zoology, meteorologist and geology), naval seamen
- An army officer to care for the ponies
- Professional photographer and film expert
- Intention to bring 25 men
- Other staff: cook, electrician, carpenter, boat handler, mechanic, doctor

Appendix 4

'Hold Fast to Dreams'
by The Unknown Poet

Hold fast your dreams,
they shelter you through lonely nights,
gently they become the pillow,
that puts destination in your sights.

Hold tight the memories,
the heart ache that burns,
for the one who wins,
is the one who remembers and learns.

Nurture the moments,
handle with care,
for destiny states,
for each heart there's a pair.

Cast off the anger,
and its deep rooted seed,
remember 'twas anger,
that caused your heart to bleed,

Snuggle each memory
a warm blanket held tight,
bringing your vision, guidance and sunlight.

Push away despair, nurture the hope,
so impossible it seems,
but the only way out,
is to hold fast to dreams.

BIBLIOGRAPHY

Bibliography

Abbs, P. (1987) *Living Powers: The Arts in Education*. Hampshire: Falmer Press

Abbs, P. (1994) *The Educational Imperative*. London: Falmer Press.

Ackroyd, J. (2000) *Literacy Alive*. London: Hodder & Stoughton.

Ackroyd-Pilkington, J. (2001) 'Acting, Representation and Role', *Research in Drama Education*, 6, 9–22.

Berry, C. (1993) *The Actor and the Text*. London: Virgin Books. Revised edition.

Best, D. (1992) *The Rationality of Feeling*. London: The Falmer Press.

Boal, A. (1992) *Games for Actors and non Actors* (translated by A. Jackson). London: Routledge.

Boal, A. (1995) *Rainbow of Desire*. London: Routledge.

Bolton, G. (1979) *Towards a Theory of Drama in Education*. London: Longman.

Bolton, G. (1984) *Drama as Education*. London: Longman.

Bolton, G. (1992) *New Perspectives on Classroom Drama*. Hemel Hempstead: Simon & Schuster.

Bolton, G. (1998) *Acting in Classroom Drama*. Stoke-on-Trent: Trentham Books.

Bolton, G. and Heathcote, D. (1999) *So You Want to Use Role Play?* Stoke-on-Trent: Trentham Books.

Bowell, P. and Heap, B.S. (2001) *Planning Process Drama*. London: David Fulton Publishers.

Bruner, J. (1966) *Towards a Theory of Instruction*. Cambridge, MA: Harvard University Press.

Bruner, J. (1978) *The Process of Education*. Cambridge, MA: Harvard University Press.

Carey, J. (1995) 'Drama: One Forum Many Voices' *The Journal of National Drama*, 3, 25–28.

Department of Education and Science, (1999) *Drama, Arts Education, Teachers Guidelines*. Dublin: The Stationery office.

Drummond, J. and Pollard, A. (1998) *Exploring Play in the Early Years*. London: David Fulton Publishers.

Eisner, E. (2002) *The Arts and the Creation of Mind*. New Haven & London: Yale University Press.

Esslin, M. (1987) *The Field of Drama*. London: Methuen.

Fleming, M. (1994) *Starting Drama Teaching*. London: David Fulton Publishers.

Fleming, M. (1997) *The Art of Drama Teaching*. London: David Fulton Publishers.

Fleming, M. (2001) *Teaching Drama in the Primary and Secondary School*. London: David Fulton Publishers.

Foster, J. (1977) *The Influences of Rudolf Laban*. London: Lepus Books.

Foster, R. (1976) *Knowing in my Bones*. London: A&C Black.

Freire, P. (1970) *Pedagogy of the Oppressed*. London: Penguin.

Gibson, R. (1982) 'The Education of Feeling' in Abbs, P. (1989) ed., T*he Symbolic Order: a Contemporary Reader for the Arts Debate*. London: Falmer Press.

Green, M. (1995) *Releasing the Imagination*. San Francisco: Jossey Bass.

Gura, P. (ed.) (1992) *Exploring Learning: Young Children and Blockplay*. London: Paul Chapman.

Harrington, J.P. (Ed.) (1991) *Modern Irish Drama: A Norton Critical Anthology*. New york: Norton.

Heaney, M. (2000) *The Names upon the Harp*. London: Faber and Faber.

Heathcote, D. (1984) *Dorothy Heathcote: Collected Writings on Education and Drama* (eds. L. Johnson and C. O'Neill). London: Hutchinson.

Hendy, L. & Toon, L. (2001) *Supporting Drama and Imaginative Play in the Early Years*. Buckingham: Open University Press.

Hodgson, J. and Richards, E. (1966) *Improvisation*. Whiststable: Latimer Trend & Co. Ltd.

Hornbrook, D. (1998a) *Education and Dramatic Art*. London: Blackwell Education. First Edition published in 1989.

Hornbrook, D. (1998b) *On the Subject of Drama*. London: Routledge.

Jackson, T. (Ed.) (1993). *Learning through Theatre*. London and New York: Routledge.

Johnston, K. (1981) *Impro: Improvisation and the Theatre*. London: Methuen.

Kempe, A. (1988) *The Drama Sampler*. Oxford: Basil Blackwell.

Kempe, A. (1990) *The GCSE Course Book*. Oxford: Basil Blackwell.

Kempe, A. and Lockwood, M. (2000) *Drama in and out of the Literacy Hour*. Reading: The Reading and Language Information Centre.

Kempe, A. and Nicholson, H. (2001) *Learning to Teach Drama 11–18*. London: Continuum.

Kempe, A. and Warner, L. (1997) *Starting with Scripts*. Cheltenham: Stanley Thomas.

Laban, R. (1948) *Modern Educational Dance*. London: Macdonald and Evans.

Lacey, S., & Woolland, B. (1992) 'Educational Drama and Radical Theatre Practice', *New Theatre Quarterly*, Vol. 8 No: 29, 81–91.

Langer, S. (1953) *Feeling and Form*. London: Routledge, Kegan and Paul.

Lyas, C. (1997) *Aesthetics*. London: UCL Press.

McArdle, J. (1998) *Flying on Both Wings*. Dublin, National Theatre.

McCullough, C. (ed.) (1998) *Theatre Praxis, Teaching through Theatre Practice*. London: MacMillan.

Mitter, S. (1992) *Systems of Rehearsals*. London: Routledge.

Moore, S., (1976) *The Stanislavsky System*. New York: Penguin.

Morgan, N. and Saxton, J. (1991) *Teaching Drama*. London: Hutchinson.

Moyles, J.R. (1989) *Just Playing? The Role and Status of Play in Early Childhood Education*. Milton Keynes: Open University Press.

Moyles, J.R. (1991) *Play as a Learning Process in Your Classroom*. London: Mary Glasgow.

Neelands, J. (1984) *Making Sense of Drama*. Oxford: Heinemann.

Neelands, J. (1990) *Structuring Drama Work* (ed. T. Goode). Cambridge University Press.

Neelands, J. (1992) *Learning through Imagined Experience*. London: Hodder & Stoughton.

Neelands, J. (1998) *Beginning Drama 11–14*. London: David Fulton Publishers.

Neelands, J. and Dobson, W. (2000) *Drama and Theatre Studies at AS/A Level*. London: Hodder & Stoughton.

Nicholson, J. (2000) *Teaching Drama 11–18*. London: Continuum.

O'Neill and Lambert, (1982) *Drama Structures*. London: Hutchinson & Co.

O'Neill, C. (1995) *Drama Worlds, A Framework for Process Drama*. Portsmouth: Heinemann.

O'Toole, J. (1992) *The Process of Drama: Negotiating Art and Meaning*. Abingdon: Routledge.

Paley, V.G. (2004) *A Child's Work, the Importance of Fantasy Play*. London: The University of Chicago Press.

Piaget, J. (1951) *Play, Dreams and Imitation in Childhood*. London: Institute for Public Policy Research.

Piaget, J. (1965) *The Moral Development of the Child*. New York: The Free Press.

Poulter, C. (1987) *Playing the Game*. Hampshire: Palgrave Macmillan.

Resources Pull-Out (*Drama* Vol. 3, no. 3, 1995)*

Richards, T. (1995) *At Work with Grotowski on Physical Actions*. London: Routledge.

Sayeed, Z. and Guerin, E. (2000) *Early Years Play*. London: David Fulton Publishers.

Singer, D. and Singer, J. (1990) *The House of Make-believe*. Cambridge, MA: Harvard University Press.

Slade, P. (1995) *Child Play, its Importance for Human Development*. London: Jessica Kinsley Publishers.

Smith, M. (2002) *An Unsung Hero: The Remarkable Story of Tom Crean – Antarctic Survivor*. London: Headline Book Publishing Ltd.

Smilansky, S. (1968) *The Effects of Socio-dramatic Play on Disadvantaged Pre-school Children*. New York: Wiley.

Smith-Autard, J. (2002) *The Art of Dance in Education*. London: A&C Black.

Stanislavsky, C., (1936) *An Actor Prepares*. London: Methuen.

Stanislavsky, C. (1981) *Creating a Role*. London: Methuen.

Toye and Prenderville (2000) *Drama and Traditional Story for the Early Years*. London & New York: Falmer.

Vygotsky, L.S. (1978) *Mind in Society*. Cambridge, MA: Harvard University Press.

Wagner, B.J. (1979) *Dorothy Heathcote; Drama as Learning Medium*. London: Hutchinson & Co.

Wangh, S. (2000) *An Acrobat of the Heart*. New York: Vintage.

Wilhelm, J. and Edminston, B. (1998) *Imaging to Learn*. Portsmouth: Heinemann.

Winston, J. and Tandy, M. (1998) *Beginning Drama: 4–11*. London: David Fulton Publishers.

Woolland, B. (1993) *The Teaching of Drama in the Primary School*. New York: Addison Wesley Longman Limited.

INDEX

Index